iCONLOGiC™

"Skills and Drills" Learning

Version: v060920
Page Count: 188
9781944607630 (Print Book & PDF)
9781944607647 (eBook)

TechSmith Camtasia 2020:
The Essentials

"Skills and Drills" Learning

Kevin Siegel

"Skills and Drills" Learning

Contents

iCONLOGiC

"Skills and Drills" Learning

About This Book

This Section Contains Information About:

The Author

Kevin Siegel is a Certified Master Trainer (CMT), Certified Technical Trainer (CTT+), and Certified Online Training Professional (COTP). Following a successful tour of duty with the U.S. Coast Guard (where Kevin was twice decorated with the Coast Guard's Achievement Medal), he has spent decades as a technical communicator, classroom and online trainer, eLearning developer, publisher, and public speaker. Kevin, who founded IconLogic, Inc., in the early 1990s, has written hundreds of training books for adult learners. Some of his best-selling books include "Adobe Captivate: The Essentials," "Articulate Storyline: The Essentials," and "TechSmith Camtasia: The Essentials." Kevin has also been recognized by Adobe as one of the top trainers worldwide.

IconLogic's Services

Founded in 1992, IconLogic is a training, development, and publishing company offering services to clients across the globe.

As a **training** company, IconLogic has directly trained tens of thousands of professionals both on-site and online on dozens of applications. Clients include some of the largest companies in the world, including Adobe Systems, Inc., Urogen, Agilent, Sanofi Pasteur, Kelsey Seybold, FAA, Office Pro, Adventist Health Systems, AGA, AAA, Wells Fargo, VA.gov, American Express, Lockheed Martin, General Mills, Grange Insurance, Electric Boat, Michigan.gov, Freddie Mac, Fannie Mae, ADP, ADT, Federal Reserve Bank of Richmond, Walmart, Kroger, Duke Energy, USCG, USMC, Canadian Blood, PSA, Department of Homeland Security, and the Department of Defense.

As a **development** company, IconLogic has produced eLearning and technical documentation for Duke Energy, World Bank, Heineken, EverFi, Bank of America, Fresenius Kabi, Wells Fargo, Federal Express, Fannie Mae, American Express, Microsoft, Department of For-Hire Vehicles, DC Child and Family Services, DCORM, Canadian Blood, Cancer.org, MLB, Archrock, NEEF, CHUBB, Canadian Natural Resources, and Hagerty Insurance.

As a **publishing** company, IconLogic has published hundreds of critically acclaimed books and created technical documents for both print and digital publication. Some of the most popular titles over the years include books on HTML, Dreamweaver, QuarkXPress, PageMaker, InDesign, Word, Excel, Access, Publisher, RoboHelp, RoboDemo, iSpring, Presenter, Storyline, Captivate, and PowerPoint for eLearning.

You can learn more about IconLogic's varied services at www.iconlogic.com.

Book Conventions

In our experience, humans learn best by doing, not just by watching or listening. With this concept in mind, instructors and authors with years of experience training adult learners have created IconLogic books. IconLogic books typically contain a minimal amount of text and are loaded with hands-on activities, screen captures, and challenge exercises to reinforce newly acquired skills. This book is divided into modules. Because each module builds on lessons learned in a previous module, it is recommended that you complete each module in succession.

Lesson Key

Instructions for you to follow look like this:

❑ choose **File > Open**

If you are expected to type anything or if something is important, it is set in bold type like this:

❑ type **9** into the text field

If you are expected to press a key on your keyboard, the instruction looks like this:

❑ press [**shift**]

Confidence Checks

As you work through this book, you will come across the image at the right (which indicates a Confidence Check). Throughout each module, you are guided through hands-on, step-by-step activities. To help ensure that you are understanding the book's content, Confidence Checks encourage you to complete a process or steps on your own (without step-by-step guidance). Because some of the book's activities build on completed Confidence Checks, you should complete each of the Confidence Checks in order.

Software & Asset Requirements

To complete the lessons presented in this book, you will need TechSmith Camtasia **version 2020** for the Mac or PC installed on your computer. Camtasia does not come with this book, but a free trial version can be downloaded from TechSmith.com.

You will need to download free project assets (data files) that have been created specifically to support this book and this version of Camtasia (see the "Project Files" section below).

You'll be hearing audio throughout the lessons, so you'll either need a headset or speakers. And you'll be recording your own voiceover audio, so you'll need some sort of microphone.

You will learn how to incorporate Microsoft PowerPoint presentations into Camtasia projects. To complete those activities, you will need a recent version of PowerPoint.

Camtasia 2020 Project Assets

To help you get started with mastering Camtasia, I've provided you all of the assets you need to get started except Camtasia 2020. I call these assets data files, and they include several Camtasia projects, videos, images, and audio files. The step-by-step instructions for downloading the data files are on the next page.

As you work through this book, pretend that you work for Super Simplistic Solutions, a fictional company in Anytown, USA. As the lead corporate trainer, your job is to create all of the eLearning for Super Simplistic Solutions using TechSmith Camtasia 2020.

Download and Extract the Data Files

1. Download the support files that accompany this book.

   ❑ start a web browser and go to the following website: **http://www.iconlogic.com**

   ❑ from the top right of the page, click the **Data Files** link

   ❑ depending on your platform, click either **PC** or **Macintosh**

   ❑ from the **TechSmith Camtasia Data Files** area, click the **Camtasia 2020: The Essentials** link

Techsmith Camtasia Data Files

- Camtasia 2020: The Essentials
- Camtasia 2019: The Essentials

  Camtasia 2020 The Essentials Data Files
- Camtasia 2019: The Essentials ZIP file

The download is a zipped file containing several folders and files. On most web browsers, a dialog box opens asking if you want to Save or Open the file. The image below is the dialog box you'll likely see if you use Mozilla Firefox.

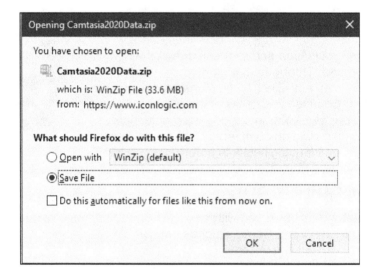

2. Save the file to your desktop.

3. Once the file has successfully downloaded, close the web browser.

4. Locate the **Camtasia2020Data.zip** file you downloaded to your computer.

5. Unzip the downloaded file.

   I suggest extracting the zipped file to your desktop. Once unzipped, there should be a folder on your computer named **Camtasia2020Data**.

How TechSmith Software Updates Affect This Book

This book was written specifically to teach you how to use TechSmith Camtasia **version 2020**. At the time this book was written, Camtasia 2020 was the latest and greatest version of Camtasia available from TechSmith.

With each major release of Camtasia, my intention is to write a new book to support that version and make it available within 30-60 days of the software being released by TechSmith. From time to time, TechSmith makes updates of Camtasia available for customers that fix bugs or add functionality. For instance, I would expect TechSmith to update Camtasia with a patch or two within a few months of Camtasia 2020 being released. That patched version might be called Camtasia **2020.0.1** or perhaps **2020.1**. You can check your Camtasia version by choosing **Help > About Camtasia** if you're on a PC; **Camtasia 2020 > About Camtasia** if you're on a Mac.

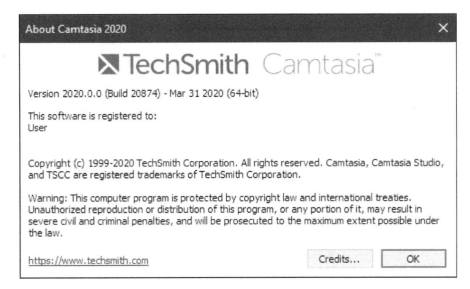

The updates from TechSmith are usually bug fixes and have little to no impact on the lessons presented in this book. However, TechSmith sometimes makes significant changes to the way Camtasia looks or behaves, even with minor updates. For instance, when TechSmith updated Camtasia from version 8.3 to 8.4, several features were changed throwing readers of my books into a tizzy.

Because it is not possible for me to recall and update printed books, some instructions you are asked to follow in this book may not match the patched/updated version of Camtasia that you might be using. If something on your screen does not match what is showing in the book, please visit the Errata page on the IconLogic website (http://www.iconlogic.com/skills-drills-workbooks/errata-pages-return-policy.html or contact me directly at ksiegel@iconlogic.com).

Contacting IconLogic

Web: **www.iconlogic.com**
Phone: **888.812.4827**
Email: **ksiegel@iconlogic.com**

Notes

iCONLOGiC

"Skills and Drills" Learning

Rank Your Skills

Before starting this book, complete the skills assessment on the next page.

Skills Assessment

How this assessment works

Below you will find 10 course objectives for *TechSmith Camtasia 2020: The Essentials*. **Before starting the book:** Review each objective and rank your skills using the scale next to each objective. A rank of ① means **No Confidence** in the skill. A rank of ⑤ means **Total Confidence**. After you've completed this assessment, go through the entire book. **After finishing the book:** Review each objective and rank your skills now that you've completed the book. Most people see dramatic improvements in the second assessment after completing the lessons in this book.

Before-Class Skills Assessment

1.	I can add media to the Media Bin.	①	②	③	④	⑤
2.	I can add a Quiz to a Project.	①	②	③	④	⑤
3.	I can create Captions.	①	②	③	④	⑤
4.	I can share Camtasia projects on YouTube.	①	②	③	④	⑤
5.	I can record voiceover audio within Camtasia.	①	②	③	④	⑤
6.	I can add objects to a project from the Library.	①	②	③	④	⑤
7.	I can create an animation with Behaviors.	①	②	③	④	⑤
8.	I can edit an audio file within Camtasia.	①	②	③	④	⑤
9.	I can upload content to Screencast.com.	①	②	③	④	⑤
10.	I can record screen actions using the Recorder.	①	②	③	④	⑤

After-Class Skills Assessment

1.	I can add media to the Media Bin.	①	②	③	④	⑤
2.	I can add a Quiz to a Project.	①	②	③	④	⑤
3.	I can create Captions.	①	②	③	④	⑤
4.	I can share Camtasia projects on YouTube.	①	②	③	④	⑤
5.	I can record voiceover audio within Camtasia.	①	②	③	④	⑤
6.	I can add objects to a project from the Library.	①	②	③	④	⑤
7.	I can create an animation with Behaviors.	①	②	③	④	⑤
8.	I can edit an audio file within Camtasia.	①	②	③	④	⑤
9.	I can upload content to Screencast.com.	①	②	③	④	⑤
10.	I can record screen actions using the Recorder.	①	②	③	④	⑤

IconLogic, Inc.
www.iconlogic.com | info@iconlogic.com

iCONLOGiC

"Skills and Drills" Learning

Preface

In This Module You Will Learn About:

Planning eLearning Lessons

If you want to create eLearning, Camtasia is an essential development tool. However, if your goal is effective and relevant eLearning, consider the following:

☐ **Why are you creating an eLearning course?** You'd be surprised how many people start Camtasia and just start creating content. This kind of development process might be well intentioned, but you really need to map out the entire course, including the way you are going to track learner comprehension (if that's important to you). During the mapping process, you might conclude that your course isn't appropriate for eLearning and move on to another course.

☐ **Who is your audience?** The way children learn is different from adults. For instance, children need praise and encouragement during the learning process; however, adult learners might find such praise and encouragement annoying.

☐ **What exactly are you teaching, and is it appropriate for eLearning?** Not every lesson in an instructor-led course can be effectively re-tooled for eLearning. For instance, if a course relies on breakout groups, group discussion, or collaborative work, those aspects of the course cannot easily be included in Camtasia. Keep in mind that learners almost always work on their own with little or no interaction with a colleague.

☐ **Does your project need closed captions?** If the answer is yes, you should budget approximately 10-15 percent more time to create closed captions in your project.

☐ **Do you want your projects to contain images, videos, and background music?** If so, where will you get them? Camtasia includes a robust number of assets in the Library, and there are more assets available via a subscription plan to TechSmith. Also, are you going to use a template? If so, who is going to design and create the template?

☐ **Will there be annotations (written instructions and descriptions)?** If so, who will write the content for the annotations?

Do you need a storyboard?

Do you need an eLearning script?

Do you need a voiceover script?

☐ **Is your course soft skills, or is it a video demonstration?** If it is soft skills, does it make sense to create most of the content in Microsoft PowerPoint and then import the presentation into Camtasia?

eLearning Development Phases

The infographic below offers a visual way to think about the eLearning development process and phases. A larger version of the graphic can be downloaded from www.iconlogic.com/skills-drills-workbooks/elearning-resources.html.

eLearning Development Phases

DISCOVERY

Meet with the client. Find out **what they want** in an ideal eLearning course. Who is the **audience**? Define a course **mission statement** for the course in general. You'll also need a mission statement for each lesson in the course. Will the course require **accessibility**? **Audio**? Will it need to be **localized**? What kind of **hardware** will students be using to access the course?

DESIGN

Which tool will you be using to develop the content (**Camtasia, Captivate, Presenter, Storyline**, or perhaps a combination of a couple tools)? **Instructional design**, a **graphical treatment**, and **navigational choices** are now made and implemented.

WRITING and/or STORYBOARDING

Now that you have chosen a production tool and decided the overall design of the course, you'll need to **plot out the flow** of the course and **write a script and/or a storyboard**. If the course includes voiceover audio, you'll need a separate (and different) script for that.

PRODUCTION

Now it's time to get busy with the **development work** in the selected tool. This includes everything right up to the point of publishing. You'll also **beta test** the lessons in this phase as they are completed.

CLIENT APPROVAL

You're almost there! But, before project completion, you'll need to get your **client's approval**. Depending upon how this goes, **you may need to repeat** parts of **steps two, three, and four**.

PUBLISHING and IMPLEMENTATION

This includes not only **publishing locally**, but uploading the content to a **web server** or **LMS (SCORM or AICC)**. Be sure to allow time to work out bugs in this phase.

MAINTENANCE

You did a great job! But sometimes changes and updates are necessary. This phase includes **making updates** to the content and **re-posting to the LMS or web server**.

Brought to you by:

iCONLOGiC
www.iconlogic.com

Camtasia Production Times (Level of Effort)

When I say production time, I'm referring to the actual time you will spend adding content to the Media Bin, adding that content to the Timeline, adding animations, annotations, etc. It may sound like common sense, but the longer the play time for your videos, the longer it will typically take for you to produce them in Camtasia.

Many new developers underestimate the number of hours needed to produce eLearning. Consider the following guide.

Project Size	Number of Production Hours
Small Videos (1-3 minutes of play time)	1-6 hours
Medium Videos (4-6 minutes)	8-12 hours
Long Videos (7-10 minutes)	14-20 hours
Extra-Long Videos (more than 10 minutes)	Consider splitting videos this large into smaller Camtasia projects.

Project Size and Display Resolution

Several years ago, monitors were small and display resolutions low. A display resolution of 800 x 600 pixels was common. If you developed eLearning content for a display that small, a Camtasia canvas size of 640 x 480 worked well.

A few years later, 1024 x 768 was the standard display resolution, resulting in typical Camtasia projects sized to 800 x 600.

According to **w3schools.com**, a typical desktop screen resolution today is 1366 x 768, and it's trending higher.

What's the ideal size for a Camtasia project? Unfortunately, there isn't a cookie-cutter answer. The width and height of a software demonstration you record depends largely on the size of your display, your display resolution, and the software you're recording (some software cannot be resized and may need to take up your entire display).

Video cards and display sizes vary from computer to computer. I want my course recordings to look consistent, so I always use the same computer, same resolution, same template, and same size Camtasia recording area.

In the image at the right, notice the suggested Canvas Dimensions available in Camtasia 2020.

According to TechSmith, if you are creating content for learners on Instagram, consider a Canvas size of 640 x 640. FaceBook video? Think 820 x 462. YouTube? Consider a project size of 1920 x 1080 or 1280 x 720.

If your target audience uses mobile devices or widescreen displays, widescreen dimensions such as 720p work well.

Design Best Practices

Much of what you do in Camtasia will feel similar to what you can do in Microsoft PowerPoint. If you've used PowerPoint, you are familiar with adding objects to a slide. In Camtasia, you add objects to the Canvas and use the Timeline to control when those objects are seen by the learner. Unlike PowerPoint, which can contain hundreds of slides, there is only one Canvas in Camtasia, and only one Timeline.

You don't have to be a seasoned designer to produce beautiful and effective Camtasia projects. Here are a few tips to get you started:

☐ If you're creating the content in PowerPoint, there are occasions when a bulleted list is the best way to convey an idea. Although PowerPoint uses a bulleted approach to information by default, you do not have to use that format in eLearning.

☐ Try splitting the bullets into separate slides with a single image to illustrate each point, or forgo the text and replace it with a chart, diagram, or other informative/interesting image.

☐ It is not necessary to have every bit of information you cover on the screen at one time. Encourage your audience to listen and, if necessary, take notes based on what you say, not what is shown on the screen.

☐ Few learners are impressed with how many moving, colorful objects each slide contains. When it comes to eLearning, the old saying "content is King" has never been more appropriate. Ensure each of your screens contains relevant, need-to-know information and that the information is presented as clutter-free as possible.

☐ Consider taking more of a photographic approach to the images you use. You can easily find stock photographs on the web using any one of a number of pay-for-use websites. There are many free sites, but keep in mind that to save time and frustration (and improve on the selection and quality), you might want to set aside a budget to pay for images.

Fonts and eLearning

The most important thing about eLearning is solid content. But could you be inadvertently making your content harder to read and understand by using the wrong fonts? Is good font selection really important? Read on to discover the many surprising ways fonts can affect your content.

Some Fonts Read Better On-Screen

eCommerce Consultant Dr. Ralph F. Wilson did a study in 2001 to determine if serif fonts (fonts with little lines on the tops and bottoms of characters, such as Times New Roman) or sans serif fonts (those without lines, such as Arial) were more suited to being read on computer monitors. His study concluded that although Times New Roman is easily read in printed materials, the lower resolution of monitors (72 dots per inch (dpi) versus 180 dpi or higher) makes it much more difficult to read in digital format. Times New Roman 12 pt was pitted against Arial 12 pt with respondents finding the sans serif Arial font more readable at a rate of two to one.

Lorem ipsum frangali puttuto rigali fortuitous confulence magficati alorem. Lorem ipsum frangali puttuto rigali fortuitous confulence magficati alorem.	Lorem ipsum frangali puttuto rigali fortuitous confulence magficati alorem. Lorem ipsum frangali puttuto rigali fortuitous confulence magficati alorem.
Times New Roman 12 pt	Arial 12 pt
520	1123
32%	68%

Source: http://www.practicalecommerce.com/articles/100159-html-email-fonts

Wilson also tested the readability of Arial versus Verdana on computer screens and found that in font sizes greater than 10 pt, Arial was more readable, whereas Verdana was more readable in font sizes 10 pt and smaller.

So should you stop using Times New Roman in your eLearning lessons? Not completely. For instance, you can use Times New Roman for text content that is not expected to be read quickly.

Some Fonts Increase Trust

A 2008 study by Sharath Sasidharan and Ganga Dhanesh for the Association of Information Systems found that typography can affect trust in eCommerce. The study found that to instill trust in online consumers, you should keep it simple: "To the extent possible, particularly for websites that need to engage in financial transactions or collect personal information from their users, the dominant typeface used to present text material should be a serif or sans serif font such as Times New Roman or Arial."

If you feel your eLearning content will be presented to a skeptical audience (or one you've never worked with before), dazzling them with fancy fonts may not be the way to go. You can use fancy fonts from time to time to break up the monotony of a dry lesson but use such nonstandard fonts sparingly. Use the fancy fonts for headings or as accents but not for the bulk of your text.

The Readability of Fonts Affects Participation

A study done at the University of Michigan in 2008 on typecase in instructions found that the ease with which a font in instructional material is read can have an impact on the perceived skill level needed to complete a task.

The study found that if directions are presented in a font that is deemed more difficult to read, the task will be viewed as being difficult, taking a long time to complete, and, perhaps, not even worth trying.

The results of the study by Wilson indicate that it is probably not a good idea to present eLearning material, especially to beginners, in Times New Roman, because it may make the information seem too difficult to process or overwhelming.

Popular eLearning Fonts

I polled my "Skills & Drills" newsletter readers and asked which fonts they tended to use in eLearning. Here is a list of the most popular fonts:

- ☐ Verdana
- ☐ Helvetica
- ☐ Arial
- ☐ Calibri
- ☐ Times
- ☐ Palatino
- ☐ Times New Roman
- ☐ Century Schoolbook (for print)

Fonts and Personas

If you are creating eLearning for business professionals, you might want to use a font that is different from one you would use if you were creating eLearning for high school students. But what font would you use if you want to convey a feeling of happiness? Formality? Cuddliness?

In a study (funded by Microsoft) by A. Dawn Shaikh, Barbara S. Chaparro, and Doug Fox, the perceived personality traits of fonts are categorized. The table below shows the top three fonts for each personality objective.

	Top Three		
Stable	TNR	Arial	Cambria
Flexible	Kristen	Gigi	Rage Italic
Conformist	Courier New	TNR	Arial
Polite	Monotype Corsiva	TNR	Cambria
Mature	TNR	Courier New	Cambria
Formal	TNR	Monotype Corsiva	Georgia
Assertive	**Impact**	**Rockwell Xbold**	Georgia
Practical	Georgia	TNR	Cambria
Creative	Gigi	Kristen	Rage Italic
Happy	Kristen	Gigi	Comic Sans
Exciting	Gigi	Kristen	Rage Italic
Attractive	Monotype Corsiva	Rage Italic	Gigi
Elegant	Monotype Corsiva	Rage Italic	Gigi
Cuddly	Kristen	Gigi	Comic Sans
Feminine	Gigi	Monotype Corsiva	Kristen
Unstable	Gigi	Kristen	Rage Italic
Rigid	**Impact**	Courier New	Agency FB
Rebel	Gigi	Kristen	Rage Italic
Rude	**Impact**	**Rockwell Xbold**	Agency FB
Youthful	Kristen	Gigi	Comic Sans
Casual	Kristen	Comic Sans	Gigi
Passive	Kristen	Gigi	Comic Sans
Impractical	Gigi	Rage Italic	Kristen
Unimaginative	Courier New	Arial	Consolas
Sad	**Impact**	Courier New	Agency FB
Dull	Courier New	Consolas	Verdana
Unattractive	**Impact**	Courier New	**Rockwell Xbold**
Plain	Courier New	**Impact**	**Rockwell Xbold**
Coarse	**Impact**	**Rockwell Xbold**	Courier New
Masculine	**Impact**	**Rockwell Xbold**	Courier New

Source: http://www.usabilitynews.org

iCONLOGiC
"Skills and Drills" Learning

Module 1: Exploring Camtasia

In This Module You Will Learn About:

And You Will Learn To:

The Camtasia Interface

During these first few guided activities, I'd like to give you a chance to familiarize yourself with Camtasia's workspace. Specifically, you'll start Camtasia, access the Getting Started project, open a project from the Camtasia2020Data folder, and poke around Camtasia's interface a bit.

Guided Activity 1: Open a Camtasia Project

1. Start Camtasia 2020.

    If this is your first time starting Camtasia, a **Getting Started** project has likely opened by default, and it's playing.

    To pause the Getting Started project preview, look to the right side of the Camtasia window, and you'll see a playbar centered just beneath the preview.

2. If necessary, click the **Pause** button.

The playback controls shown above left are from Camtasia for Windows. Above right are the playback controls for Camtasia for Mac. There's little difference between the two platforms except the controls on the Windows side include keyboard shortcuts for playback; the Mac side does not display the shortcuts. When the differences between the two platforms are subtle, as shown above, I'll rarely mention them again. When the differences are significant, I'll call them out with platform-specific steps or screen shots.

If this isn't your first time starting Camtasia or you have already created a project or two, I'm betting that the Getting Started project did not open at all. If you're curious to see the Getting Started project, you can open it at any time by choosing **Help > Open Getting Started Project**. (If the **Help** menu isn't available, you'll first need to create a New Project by clicking **New Project** on the Welcome window.)

The picture below is an example of what you will typically see the second time you start Camtasia. By default, there is a **Welcome** window on the screen.

At this point, it does not matter if a project is open. The important thing is to ensure you have started Camtasia. Also, if you have not yet downloaded the IconLogic project assets (also known as Data Files), turn to the **About This Book** section at the beginning of this book and work through the **Download and Extract the Data Files** activity on page viii.

3. Open a project from the Camtasia2020Data, Projects folder.

   ☐ if the **Welcome** window (shown above) is on your screen, click the **Open Project** button; if a Camtasia project is currently open, choose **File > Open Project**

   The **Open** dialog box appears.

   ☐ navigate to the **Camtasia2020Data** folder

   ☐ open the **Projects** folder and then open the **Demo** project

   The entire screen that you see (from the **File** menu in the upper left to the objects along the bottom of the window) is known as the **Editor**. There are several things to explore within the Editor, which you will do soon enough. First, let's see what happens if you decide to create a new project.

4. Create a new project.

☐ choose **File > New Project** (if prompted, don't save the Demo project)

You are probably used to programs that allow you to open multiple projects concurrently and switch between them. On the Mac version of Camtasia, you can switch between open projects via the Window menu. In the image below, you can see that I've created a new project on my Mac and the Demo project is still open.

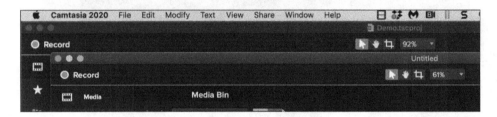

On the PC, you can have only one Camtasia project open at any one time, so the Demo project closes when the new project is created. Additionally, there is no way to have Camtasia running without having a project open.

☐ PC users only: keep the new, untitled project open

☐ Mac users only: close all open projects (but keep Camtasia running)

5. Open a recent project.

☐ PC users, choose **File > Recent Projects > Demo**

☐ Mac users, choose **File > Open Recent > Demo**

The Demo project should once again be open, ready for you to explore.

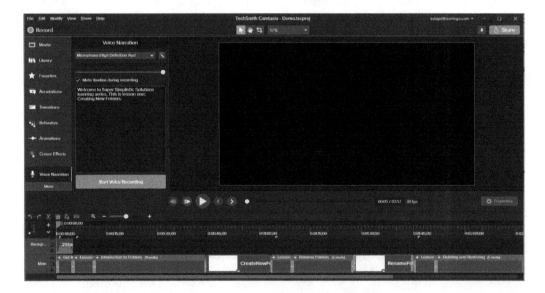

Guided Activity 2: Explore Camtasia's Tools

1. Ensure that the **Demo** project is open.

2. View the Voice Narration tool.

   ☐ choose **View > Tools > Voice Narration**

   The Voice Narration panel appears in the upper left of the Editor. The panel is used to record voice narration. You will learn to record voiceover audio beginning on page 86.

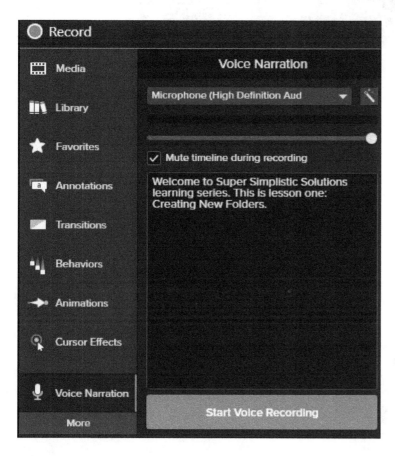

   Note: You can access all of the tools, such as Voice Narration, via the list of tools at the left. Depending upon the size of your screen, you may need to click **More** at the bottom of the list to see all of the tools.

3. Display the Annotation tools.

   ☐ from the list of tools at the left, click **Annotations**

   There are six types of Annotations that allow you to help grab the learner's attention including Callouts, Arrows & Lines, Shapes, Blur & Highlight, Sketch Motion, and Keystroke callouts. You will learn to work with Annotations beginning on page 64.

4. Display the Transition tools.

☐ from the list of tools at the left, click **Transitions**

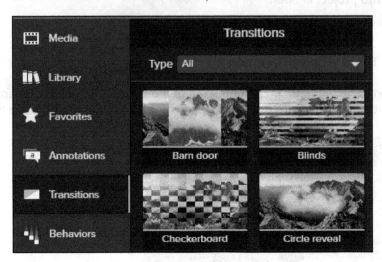

Transitions give you the ability to move from one part of your lesson to another using professional animation effects. You'll learn how to add Transitions to a project beginning on page 76.

Next you will explore the Media Bin and the Library.

The Media Bin and Library

The Media Bin and Library share one common goal: both give you access to media (images, videos, and audio) that can be added to the Camtasia Timeline. But although the Media Bin and Library share that common goal, they go about providing the assets very differently.

Let's start with the Media Bin. Every Camtasia project has its own unique Media Bin. Unfortunately, the Media Bin is empty by default. It's up to you to import assets into the Media Bin as needed. Once assets have been imported into the Media Bin, you can add the media to the Timeline. There's no limit to how many assets you can import to the Media Bin, but the bin cannot be shared or opened by other Camtasia projects.

The Library comes preloaded with dozens of free assets provided by TechSmith, including animations, icons, and music. The Library assets are available to any Camtasia project, new or old.

Guided Activity 3: Explore the Media Bin and Library

1. Ensure that the **Demo** project is open.

2. View the Media Bin.

   ☐ choose **View > Tools > Media Bin**

   There are a several assets in this project's Media Bin, including screen recordings, images, and audio.

The default view for the Media Bin is Thumbnails, which is nice if you want a decent-sized preview of the Media Bin assets. However, many developers prefer the organized look and feel of the Details view.

NOTES

3. Change the Media Bin view from Thumbnails to Details.

❑ at the bottom right of the **Media Bin,** click the **Details** icon

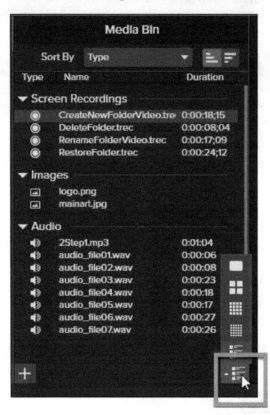

4. Change the Media Bin view from Details back to Thumbnails.

❑ at the bottom right of the Media Bin, click the **Thumbnails** icon

You will learn how to add assets to the Media Bin beginning on page 48.

5. View the Library.

❑ choose **View > Tools > Library**

The Library takes the place of the Media Bin. By default, there are several folders within the Library containing images, animations, and audio files. You can create your own folders and import your own assets into the Library. Also, there is a link at the bottom of the Library labeled "Download more assets." For $199 annually, TechSmith provides access to hundreds of thousands of royalty-free videos, images, and audio files you can use in your Camtasia project. You won't need the subscription to complete this book because you'll be using the free assets currently in the Library or within the Camtasia2020Data folder. When you start creating projects on your own and need a specific video or icon, the subscription might prove invaluable.

6. Explore Library.

   ☐ from the Library, click the triangle to the left of **Music Tracks**

   The folder opens and displays several audio files.

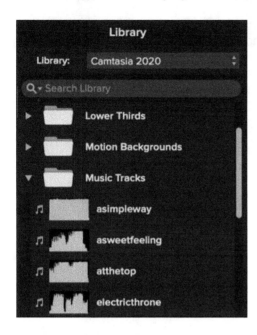

   It is simple to add any of these assets to your project—a drag and drop is all it takes. You will get a chance to do that later. For now, let's continue the Camtasia tour.

7. Preview a Library asset.

   ☐ on the **Library**, double-click any music asset

   A preview window opens, and assuming you have speakers or a headset, you will hear the music. Note that the preview windows are similar on the Mac and PC except for the location of the close window controls. The first image below is the PC preview window. The second image is the Mac preview window.

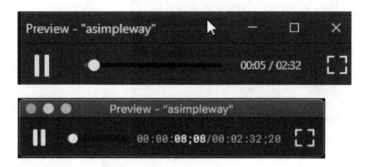

   ☐ close the Preview window

   You will learn how to add music from the Library to a project later.

The Canvas and Timeline

The Canvas, which is at the right of the Editor, offers an excellent way to position screen elements and preview the project as you're working. As you preview a project via the Canvas, you'll be able to use the Timeline to keep track of what's happening in your project and when.

The Timeline is at the bottom of the Editor. As its name implies, the Timeline is used to control the timing of objects added to the Canvas. For instance, using the Timeline, you can force objects such as images or videos to appear at the same time, or you can force one object to appear as another goes away. You'll learn to use both the Canvas and Timeline as you move through lessons in this book. For now, you'll use the Canvas to preview the assets added to the Timeline of the demo project.

Guided Activity 4: Preview a Project

1. Ensure that the **Demo** project is open.

2. Preview the project.

    ☐ below the **Canvas**, click **Play** icon

    As the lesson plays on the Canvas, notice that a thin line and strange-looking object moves across the Timeline. The object is known as the Playhead (it has both a green and a red square, which you will learn about later). The Playhead and thin line show you where the preview is at any specific point in time. You will learn to work with the Timeline as you work through the lessons in this book.

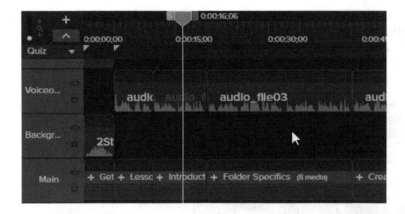

3. Detach the Canvas.

    ☐ choose **View > Canvas > Detach Canvas** (you can also find this option in the **Canvas Options** drop-down menu located just above the Canvas)

Click the menu located just above the **Canvas**) to find the **Detach Canvas** menu item.

The Canvas detaches from Editor. You can now position the panel anywhere on your display that you like.

4. Explore Full Screen Mode.

   ☐ with the Canvas detached, click the **Full Screen** button (in the lower right of the Canvas)

   While in Full Screen mode, you can see the lesson but not the Camtasia interface.

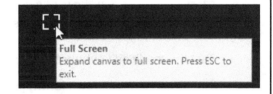

5. Exit Full Screen mode.

   ☐ press [**esc**] on your keyboard

6. Attach the Canvas.

   ☐ from the top of the detached Canvas, click the **Canvas Options** drop-down menu and choose **Attach Canvas**

   The Canvas reattaches to the upper right of the Editor.

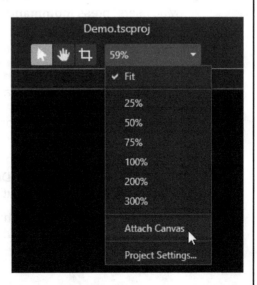

7. Use a keyboard shortcut to Zoom closer and farther away from the Canvas.

   ☐ PC users, press [**ctrl**] [=] a few times to zoom closer to the Canvas
   Mac users, press [**command**] [=] a few times to zoom closer to the Canvas

   ☐ PC users, press [**ctrl**] [-] a few times to zoom away from the Canvas
   Mac users, press [**command**] [-] a few times to zoom away from the Canvas

8. Modify the Canvas zooming keyboard shortcuts.

❏ PC users, choose **Edit > Preferences**
Mac users, choose **Camtasia 2020 > Preferences**

The Preferences dialog box opens.

❏ select the **Shortcuts** tab and then select **Canvas Options**

❏ to the right of **Zoom in on Canvas**, click the current keyboard shortcut

❏ PC users, replace the shortcut with [**ctrl**] [**shift**] [**=**]
Mac users, replace the shortcut with [**shift**] [**command**] [**=**]

Zoom in on canvas	Ctrl+Shift+=|
Zoom out on canvas	Ctrl+-
Enable/disable canvas snapping	Ctrl+;

Zoom in on canvas:	⇧⌘= ↻
Zoom out on canvas:	⌘-
Preview media outside of group:	⇧⌘G

❏ PC users, click the **OK** button
Mac users, close the Shortcuts dialog box

9. Test the modified keyboard shortcuts.

❏ PC users, press [**ctrl**] [**shift**] [**+**] a few times to zoom closer to the Canvas;
Mac users, press [**command**] [**shift**] [**+**] a few times to zoom closer to the Canvas

❏ PC users, press [**ctrl**] [**-**] a few times to zoom away from the Canvas;
Mac users, press [**command**] [**-**] to zoom away from the Canvas

10. Restore the keyboard shortcuts to their defaults.

❏ PC users, choose **Edit > Preferences**;
Mac users, choose **Camtasia 2020 > Preferences**

The Preferences dialog box reopens.

❏ select the **Shortcuts** tab

❏ PC users, click the **Restore Defaults** button
Mac users, from the **Shortcut Set** menu, choose **TechSmith Camtasia Default**

❏ PC users, click the **OK** button;
Mac users, close the Shortcuts dialog box

11. Exit Camtasia.

❏ PC users choose **File > Exit**
Mac users, choose **Camtasia 2020 > Quit**

There is no need to save any changes made to the Demo project (if prompted).

iCONLOGiC

"Skills and Drills" Learning

Module 2: Recording Videos

In This Module You Will Learn About:

- Rehearsals, page 22
- Recording Screen Actions, page 24

And You Will Learn To:

- Rehearse a Script, page 23
- Review Recording Options on the PC, page 24
- Select a Recording Area on the PC, page 29
- Create a Screen Recording on the PC, page 30
- Add a Stamp and Caption on the PC, page 32
- Add Effects While Recording on the PC, page 36
- Set Screen Recording Options on the Mac, page 38
- Specify a Mac Recording Size and Target, page 40
- Create a Screen Recording on the Mac, page 44

Rehearsals

During this module, you are going to learn how to use Camtasia to record your computer screen. Because you can use Camtasia to record just about anything you can do on your computer, I'm going to focus your efforts via the following scenario and step-by-step script:

Scenario: You have been hired to create an eLearning course that teaches new employees at your company how to use **Notepad** (if you're using Camtasia for Windows) or **TextEdit** (if you're using Camtasia for the Mac). One of the lessons you plan to record using Camtasia includes how to change the page orientation within Notepad or TextEdit.

> **Note:** Depending on your platform, Notepad or TextEdit is installed on your computer (it's a free utility). On the PC, you can find Notepad by searching for the word "Notepad." On the Mac, you can find TextEdit in the Applications folder.

Step-by-step recording script: Here are detailed, step-by-step set of instructions you would typically write yourself, or receive from a writer, a Subject Matter Expert (SME), or the instructional designer. Each step will be performed as written below in either Notepad or TextEdit.

1. Start either Notepad or TextEdit. (If using TextEdit, create a new, blank document.)

2. From within Notepad or TextEdit, click the **File** menu.

3. Click the **Page Setup** menu item.

4. Click the **Landscape** orientation button.

5. Click the **OK** button.

6. Click the **File** menu.

7. Click the **Page Setup** menu item.

8. Click the **Portrait** orientation button.

9. Click the **OK** button.

10. Stop the recording process (you're done).

The script above sounds simple. However, you will not know what kind of problems you are going to get into unless you rehearse the script prior to recording the process with Camtasia.

Let's run a rehearsal, just as if you were a big-time movie director and you were in charge of a blockbuster movie.

Places everyone, *and quiet on the set.*

Guided Activity 5: Rehearse a Script

1. Start Notepad or TextEdit.

   The process of starting either Notepad or TextEdit varies slightly depending on your operating system. If you are using Windows, click Start or the Windows button, type **notepad** and press **[enter]** to start Notepad. If you are using a Mac, choose **Go > Applications**. Double click TextEdit to open it. On the TextEdit dialog box, click **New Document** button to create a new document.

   In the images below, Notepad is pictured at the left; TextEdit is at the right.

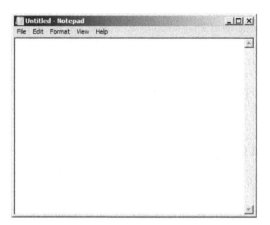 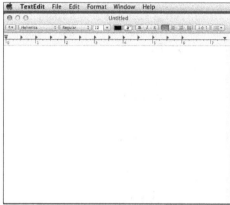

2. Rehearse the script.

   ❑ using **Notepad** or **TextEdit** (not Camtasia), click the **File** menu

   ❑ click the **Page Setup** menu item

   ❑ from the **Orientation** area, click **Landscape**

   ❑ click the **OK** button

   ❑ click the **File** menu

   ❑ click the **Page Setup** menu item

   ❑ click the **Portrait** orientation button

   ❑ click the **OK** button

   Hey, look at that! The script worked perfectly... no surprises. You are now ready to work the exact steps again. Only this time, you will record every click that you make. During the recording process, Camtasia creates a video of the entire process.

Recording Screen Actions

When you record screen actions using Camtasia, you should pretend you are using a video recorder and creating a movie (you're both the director and the producer). During the recording process, everything you do is recorded exactly as you do it. Every delay, every good click, bad click, right-click, double-click... everything is recorded. If you move your mouse too fast and race through a series of steps, the resulting video will play back the cursor speed in real time. If you move your mouse too slowly, your learners will tear their collective hairs out as they watch the cursor creep across the screen.

In the steps that follow, you'll select a recording area and then record the process of changing the Page Orientation in Notepad or TextEdit.

> **Note:** While Camtasia is similar on the Mac and PC, recording screen actions is different. On the PC, there's a separate program used for recording videos called Camtasia Recorder. On the Mac, you can record with Camtasia but there isn't a standalone Recorder program. Because recording videos in the two platforms is so different, I've split the process into two groups. PC users, your activities appear below. Mac users, skip ahead to page 38 for your activities.

Guided Activity 6: Review Recording Options on the PC

1. Start the Camtasia Recorder 2020 tool. (It can be started like any other application.)

   There are two main things to notice on your screen. First, there is a green, dashed box that is likely the size of your screen (meaning it's really big). Second, there is a control panel containing four menus (Capture, Effects, Tools, and Help).

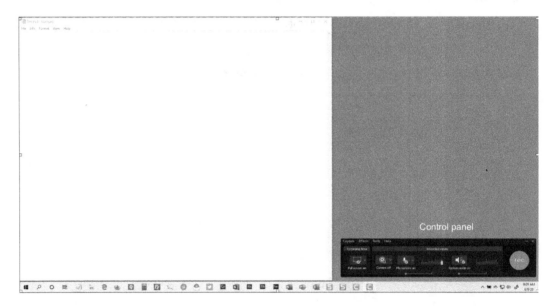

Control panel

There are two main groups on the control panel, **Recording Area** and **Recorded inputs**. There's a large, red **rec** button.

2. Review the video Capture options.

   ☐ on the **Control panel**, choose **Tools > Options**

   The Tools Options dialog box opens.

   ☐ ensure that the **General** tab is selected

   ☐ from the **Saving** area, click the **File options** button

   The File Options dialog box opens.

   ☐ from the **Output file name** area, ensure **Automatic file name** is selected

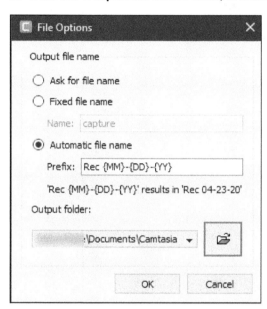

   With the **Automatic file name** option selected, you won't be prompted to name the video demo when you are finished recording. Instead, the recording will automatically be named, saved, and imported into the Camtasia Editor where it can be previewed. By default, recordings are saved to the Camtasia folder within your Documents folder.

   ☐ click the **OK** button

3. Select the Capture options.

   ☐ still working on the **General** tab, ensure your **Capture** settings match the picture below

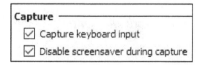

   Capture keyboard input. On by default. Camtasia captures keys as you press them on your keyboard and automatically creates annotations for you. The annotations can be edited, deleted, moved, and resized in Camtasia during production.

   Disable screen saver during capture. On by default. You should enable this option when you are creating long, unmonitored recordings.

4. Review Program options.

☐ with the Tools Options dialog box open, select the **Program** tab

☐ ensure that your options match the options shown below

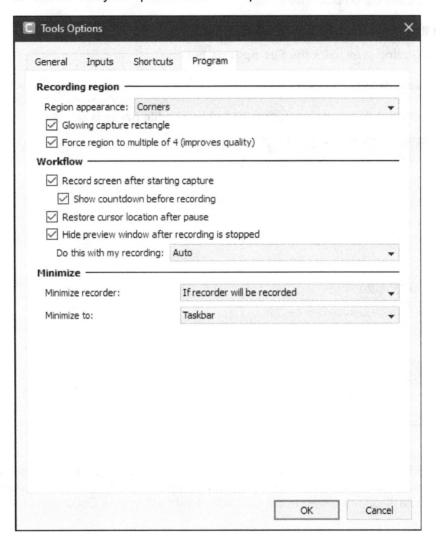

Here is what some of the options do (you can always refer to the Help menu for more information).

Glowing capture rectangle. On by default. Makes the green corners around the recording area flash.

Force region to multiple of 4. On by default. Prevents errors when viewing videos created with codecs, such as Microsoft Video 1.

Record screen after starting capture and **Show countdown before recording.** Both on by default. Once you click the Recorder's red **rec** button, the capture process begins. However, you'll have a few seconds to get ready, thanks to a countdown you will see just before the recording begins.

Restore cursor location after pause. On by default. Restores the cursor to the position on the screen prior to the pause. This allows you to seamlessly continue the action in the recording prior to the pause. You must press **[F9]** to pause and resume the recording to use this option.

Hide preview window after recording is stopped. On by default. Select this option if you don't want to preview the captured video after recording.

Minimize recorder. This prevents Camtasia from creating a video of itself.

Minimize to. By default, the recorder will be minimized to your Taskbar if it's going to be in your way during the recording process.

5. Reset the Shortcuts.

    ❑ with the **Tools Options** dialog box still open, select the **Shortcuts** tab

    ❑ click the **Restore defaults** button

    Clicking the Restore defaults button removes any previous changes made to the Shortcuts tab and resets the Shortcuts back to how they were set the day Camtasia was first installed on your computer.

6. Review the default Record/Pause keyboard shortcut.

    ❑ from the list at the left, select **Record/Pause**

    This controls the key you will press when you are ready to create your video demo.

    ❑ from the drop-down menu at the right, notice that **F9** is selected

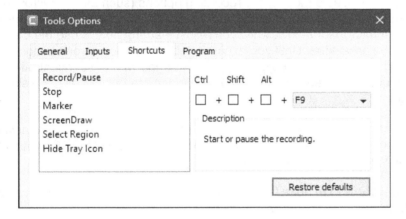

7. Review the default Stop keyboard shortcut.

    ❑ select the **Stop** option from the list at the left

    This controls the key you will press when you are finished recording your video demo.

    ❑ from the drop-down menu at the right, ensure **F10** is selected

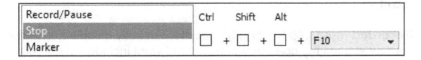

The remaining Hotkeys, although important, won't impact the video you are about to create. Understanding that [**F9**] starts or pauses the recording process and that [**F10**] stops the recording process is important to keep in mind for the activity that follows.

    ❑ click the **OK** button

8. Disable your camera and microphone.

❑ on the Recorder's Control panel, choose **Capture** and ensure that only **Record screen** is selected (remove the check mark from all of the other options)

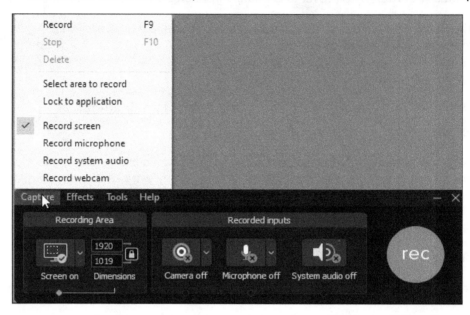

Why were you asked to disable most of the recording options (such as the microphone and your webcam)? In my experience, audio and video enhance the learner experience. However, using your microphone now, while you're just learning how to use the Camtasia Recorder, isn't such a great idea. Until you're comfortable recording screen actions, you'll likely end up having to replace the audio later. When teamed with the concentration needed to capture quality screen actions, many people tend to talk too fast, too slow, or flub the recording.

You'll learn later that it's easy to import, record, and edit audio from within Camtasia (see page 79). Once you're comfortable recording video demos, absolutely record yourself talking through the video demo down the road.

What about your webcams? I'm not a fan of "selfie videos." If you're considering capturing video of yourself, ask yourself this question: "Is my selfie video enhancing the learner experience?" The answer will likely be no.

If the answer is yes, then consider the following and perhaps you'll change your mind. Are you dressed appropriately? Yes? Okay, but what about what's behind you? Is there a poster in the background that's inappropriate? If you look good and the background is great, what about the lighting around you? What about your camera angle (is the camera pointed straight up your nose)? If you already have awesome videos of yourself, you can insert them into Camtasia later (see page 48). But I would discourage you from using your webcam at this point.

There's a final **Recorded inputs** option: **System audio**. I usually disable this feature because there are few sounds my computer makes that I want included in my recordings. However, if I was recording a virtual meeting (via Zoom or WebEx for example), I would enable System audio so that I captured the audio from the meeting.

Guided Activity 7: Select a Recording Area on the PC

1. The Camtasia Recorder should be running. In addition, the Notepad window should be open.

2. Enable screen recording.

   ❏ on the recording **Control** panel, **Recording Area**, observe the icon at left

   The icon will either display the words **Screen on** or **Screen off**.

   ❏ click the icon to toggle it to **Screen on**, if necessary

3. Lock to an application.

   ❏ click the **Screen on** drop-down menu and choose **Lock to application**

   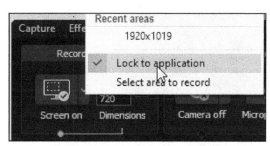

   Because Notepad is running on your computer and is within easy reach, the Camtasia Recorder grabs Notepad and makes it the recording target.

4. Set the size of the Recording Area.

   ❏ click the **Screen on** drop-down menu

   ❏ choose **720p HD (1280x720)**

   Notepad and the Recording Area resize to 1280 pixels wide and 720 pixels tall, a popular size that works well on most screens and devices.

   And now, on with the recording!

   Note: If the Recording Area is now too large for your screen, click the Screen-on drop-down menu and choose 480p SD (854x480) instead.

   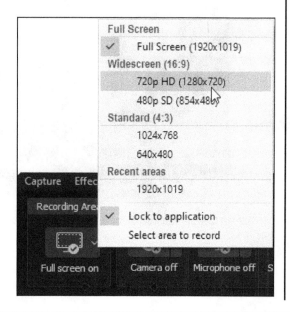

Guided Activity 8: Create a Screen Recording on the PC

1. Record a software demonstration.

   ☐ on the control panel, click the red **rec** button

   You'll see a three-second countdown.

   ☐ before the counter gets to zero, position your mouse pointer in the center of the Notepad window

   After the counter disappears, your every move (and the time it takes you to move) is being recorded.

   ☐ moving steadily (not too fast), move your mouse pointer to the **File** menu

   ☐ click the **Page Setup** menu item

   ☐ from the **Orientation** area, click **Landscape**

   ☐ click the **OK** button

   ☐ click the **File** menu

   ☐ click the **Page Setup** menu item

   ☐ click the **Portrait** orientation button

   ☐ click the **OK** button

2. Stop the recording process.

   ☐ press [**F10**] on your keyboard

   Once you press the Stop recording keyboard shortcut, the recording process terminates, and several things happen in rapid succession. First, the Camtasia Recorder application closes. Second, the Camtasia Editor opens. Third, a new project is created. The recording you created is added to the Camtasia Media Bin and inserted onto the Timeline.

If you'd like to watch the video you recorded, you can use the controls on the Canvas to play and rewind the video as you learned in the last module.

3. View the location of the recording.

    ☐ on the **Media Bin**, right-click the recording and choose **Open File Location**

    The Camtasia folder opens. By default, all of the recordings you create are saved to this folder. You can change this location in the Camtasia Recorder via **Tools > Options > Saving > File options**.

Name	Date modified	Type	Size
Custom Production Presets 20.0	4/17/20 10:11 PM	File folder	
Media	4/23/20 6:30 PM	File folder	
Rec 04-23-20.trec	4/23/20 6:30 PM	TREC File	2,284 KB

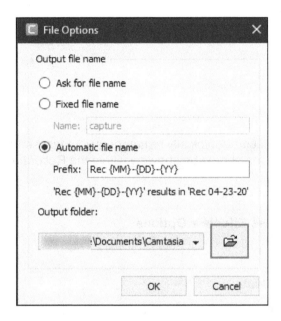

4. Close the window and return to the Camtasia project.

Recording Annotations

Annotations (informational text) can automatically be added to a Camtasia video during the recording process. There are two types of Annotation: System Stamp and Caption. Camtasia can insert one of two system stamps (time/date and elapsed time) into the recording. The stamp is imprinted into the video background (it can never be removed) and is always visible to learners. Captions are frequently used to include a copyright notice or other text message that you want to appear on the video.

Guided Activity 9: Add a Stamp and Caption on the PC

1. Ensure that you are working within the untitled Camtasia project you created during the last activity.

2. Start the Recorder from within Camtasia.

   ❑ from the top left of the **Camtasia Editor**, click **Record**

   The Camtasia Recorder reopens. The Recorder typically remembers your last settings, so unless you closed Notepad, the application should be showing within the Recording Area.

3. Add a System Stamp.

   ❑ on the Recorder control panel, choose **Effects > Options**

   The Effects Options dialog box opens.

   ❑ on the **Annotation** tab, select **Time/date**

   ❑ if necessary, deselect **Elapsed time**

   A preview of the date and time format appears in the Preview area.

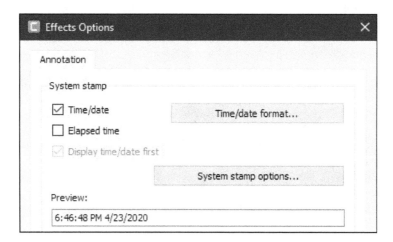

4. Specify a Time/Date Format.

❏ click the **Time/date format** button

❏ from the **Display** area, select **Date only**

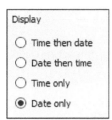

❏ click the **OK** button to return to the Effects Options dialog box

5. Set the System Stamp font.

❏ still in the Effects Options dialog box, click the **System stamp options** button

The System Stamp Options dialog box opens.

❏ click the **Font** button

❏ change the Font to **Verdana** and the Size to **10**

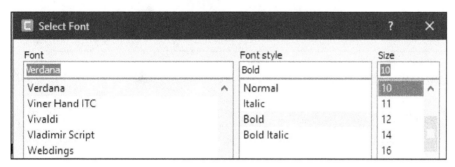

❏ click the **OK** button

You are returned to the System Stamp Options dialog box.

6. Set the System Stamp position.

❏ from the **Position** area in the upper right of the dialog box, select the lower left square (this will position the System Stamp in the lower left of your upcoming recording)

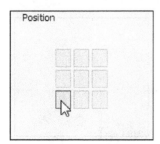

❏ click the **OK** button

You should now be back in the Effects Options dialog box.

7. Add a Caption.

❐ click in the Caption text field and type: **This is a sample lesson. Not for resale.**

❐ deselect **Prompt before capture**

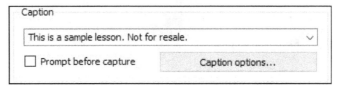

8. Set the Caption font.

❐ click the **Caption options** button

The Caption Options dialog box appears.

❐ click the **Font** button

❐ change the Font to **Verdana** and the Size to **10**

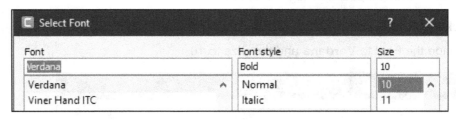

❐ click the **OK** button

9. Set the Caption Text and Background color.

❐ click the **Text color** button

The Select color dialog box opens.

❐ select any color you like

❐ click the **OK** button

❐ click the **Background color** button

The Select color dialog box opens again.

❐ select any color you like

❐ click the **OK** button

10. Set the Caption position.

❐ from the Position area, select the upper right square (this positions the Caption in the upper right of the recording)

❐ click the **OK** button twice (to close both open dialog boxes)

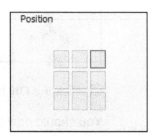

Recording Confidence Check (PC)

1. On the Recorder's Control panel, choose **Effects > Annotation > Add system stamp**.

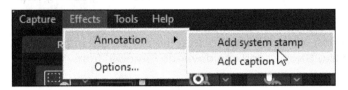

2. On the Control panel choose **Effects > Annotation > Add caption**.

   Both commands should now be selected (there should be a check mark next to both).

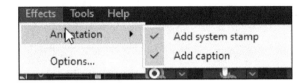

3. Click the **rec** button on the Recorder control panel.

4. Record the process of changing the page orientation like you did during your first recording session.

5. When finished, stop the recording process.

   Your new recording will be added to the Camtasia Media Bin.

6. Double-click the new recording to open a preview window.

7. Play the preview and notice that you can see both a System Stamp and Caption on the recording.

8. Close the preview window.

Recording Effects with Camtasia for Windows

Starting in the next module, you will learn how to use the Editor to add all kinds of media to an eLearning lesson that will help grab the learner's attention including text, images, and music. However, using Camtasia's Effects Toolbar, you can add several attention-grabbing visuals while you are recording your video.

> **Note:** If you add effects during the recording process, the effects are imprinted into the video background like Stamps and can never be removed from the recording.

Guided Activity 10: Add Effects While Recording on the PC

1. Ensure the Effects toolbar is enabled.

    ❏ from the top left of the Camtasia Editor, click **Record**

    The Camtasia Recorder reopens.

    ❏ on the **Control panel**, choose **Effects > Annotation** and disable both **Add system stamp** and **Add captions**

    ❏ on the **Control panel**, choose **Tools > Recording toolbars**

    The Recording Toolbars dialog box opens.

    ❏ select **Effects** and **Duration**

    ❏ click the **OK** button

2. Record a video and add screen drawings.

    ❏ click the **rec** button

    After the 3-2-1 countdown, the Effects and Duration tools should appear on the Recording toolbar (on some of my systems, the tools appear on their own; on others, I had to click in the middle of the Recording toolbar to coax the tools to appear... you may have to play with this a bit to display the tools).

    ❏ select the **ScreenDraw** tool

Drawing tools appear. You can select from among frames, lines, highlights, and a pen.

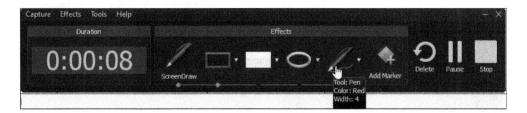

3. Select any of the tools and draw some shapes within the Notepad window.

4. When finished drawing, stop the recording.

5. Preview the video in Camtasia.

6. When finished, exit Camtasia (there is no need to save the untitled project).

7. Close the Notepad application.

   Note: The rest of this module is for Mac users only. PC users, you can skip ahead to the "Adding Media" module which begins on page 47.

Guided Activity 11: Set Screen Recording Options on the Mac

1. Change Camtasia's Preferences so that recordings open in the Editor.

   ☐ with **Camtasia 2020** running, choose **Camtasia 2020 > Preferences**

   The Preferences dialog box opens.

   ☐ from the top of the dialog box, click **Recording**

   ☐ from the **After recording** area, choose **Open in Editor**

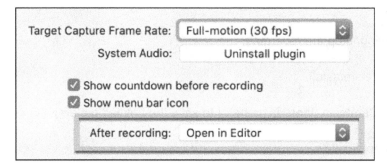

   With the **Open in Editor** option selected, your recording automatically opens in the Camtasia Editor once you stop the recording process.

2. Change the Preferences so that recordings are not automatically deleted.

   ☐ from the **Save recordings to** area, remove the check mark from **Delete after**

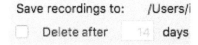

   With **Delete after** disabled, older recordings won't be automatically deleted from your computer. Assuming you've backed up your projects, you should manually empty older recordings from the Camtasia 2020 folder from time to time.

The remaining Recording options should match the image below.

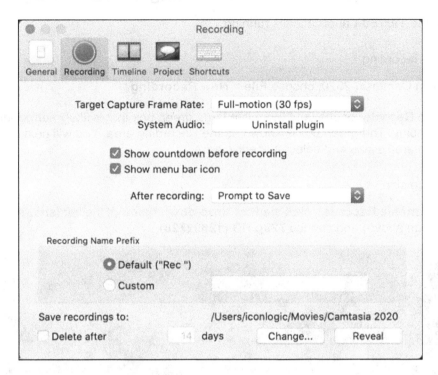

The two most important default Preferences that you did not change are **Target Capture Frame Rate** and **Show countdown before recording**.

By default, recordings are captured at 30 frames-per-second (30 fps). The higher the frame rate, the smoother a recorded video will be. However, when captured at a high frame rate, the file size of a video can be huge (especially if you record for more than a few minutes). If you find that your videos are excessive, you can experiment with lowering the frame rate prior to recording (which will lower the size of your recording, but could also lower the quality of the video).

Having the **Show countdown** option turned on is a good default. Without this option enabled, the recording process will begin the instant you click the Start Recording button... so fast you'll possibly find yourself unprepared and make mistakes while recording.

Note: If your **System Audio** area shows **Install plugin** instead of **Uninstall plugin** as shown above, click the button. When asked **Do you want to install the system Audio Plugin?**, click **Install**.

3. Review the keyboard shortcut needed to stop the recording.

   ❏ from the top of the Preferences dialog box, click **Shortcuts**

   ❏ from the list at the left, select **Recorder Options**

   ❏ at the right, notice that the **Stop recording** shortcut is [**option**] [**command**] [**2**]

Start/pause recording:	⇧⌘2
Stop recording:	⌥⌘2

4. Close the Preferences dialog box.

Guided Activity 12: Specify a Mac Recording Size and Target

1. Ensure that the **TextEdit** application is running.

2. Create a new recording.

    ☐ from within Camtasia 2020, choose **File > New Recording**

    The Camtasia Recorder opens, and there is a large green box that is likely surrounding your entire display. The green box is known as the Recording area. You will next change the Recording area's size and select a specific area.

3. Set a recording size.

    ☐ on the **Camtasia Recorder**, click the **first drop-down menu** at the left (shown circled in the image above) and choose **720p HD (1280x720)**

The recording area is now a green, dashed line. You will next specify the area of your screen as the Recording Area. In this instance, the Recording Area you need is the TextEdit application (including TextEdit's menu bar and application window).

If you have a small screen or low resolution, 1280x720 may be too large of a recording area for you. You can manually resize the capture area to any size that works best using a corner resizing handle like the one shown circled in the image below.

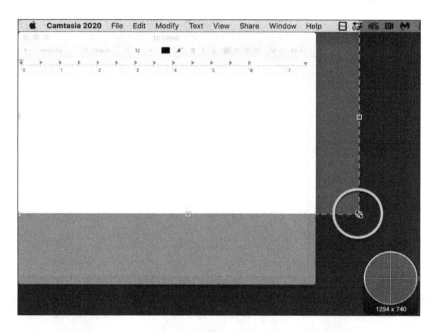

4. Set up the recording target and area.

☐ to ensure that you record the TextEdit menus, move the TextEdit application window so that it is located in the upper left-hand corner of your monitor

☐ drag the **middle** of the Camtasia Recording Area so that the upper left of the area begins in the TextEdit menu bar similar to the image below

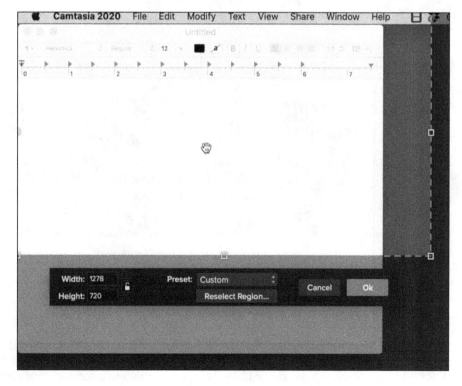

☐ click the **OK** button

5. Ensure the TextEdit window size and the Recording Area match.

☐ resize the TextEdit application window as necessary so that the TextEdit window fits nicely within the Camtasia Recording Area

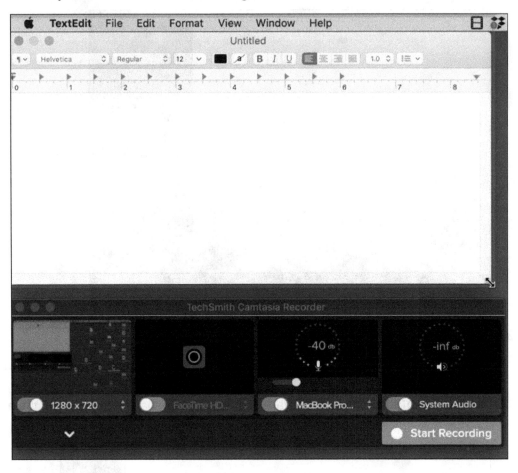

6. On the Camtasia Recorder, disable the Webcam, Microphone, and System Audio.

Why were you just instructed to disable the Webcam and audio recording features? I'm a fan of including voiceover audio in eLearning. In my experience, voiceover audio almost always enhances the learner experience. The dilemma is whether you should record the audio and the video now or add the audio to the video later in the Editor.

If you are creating micro-learning (very short videos used as "just-in-time learning"), you might want the more informal, natural feel of audio narration recorded while you click through a software process. On the other hand, if you are creating a longer, more formal course, you may want a more formal sound. In this case, I would encourage you to either hire professional talent or record your own voice in a studio and with high-quality equipment.

With some practice, you can record your voice with the Camtasia Recorder while you're creating the video. Or you can record your voice in the Camtasia Editor while you are producing the video. (You will learn how to record and edit audio in Camtasia beginning on page 79). You can also record your voice separately, using any number of audio editing tools such as Audacity, Sound Forge, or Adobe Audition, and import the audio files into the Camtasia Media Bin.

What about capturing yourself with your webcam? Ask yourself this question: "Is it really necessary to insert myself into the course?" The answer will likely be no.

If you do elect to record yourself, are you sure you're dressed appropriately? What about what's behind you? Is there a poster in the background that's inappropriate? If you look good and the background is great, what about the lighting around you? What about your camera angle?

Because there's much to consider when it comes to selfie-videos, consider not doing them. Besides, if you have awesome existing videos of yourself, you can insert them into Camtasia later (see page 48).

But enough about all that. Let's go ahead and record your first software demonstration.

Guided Activity 13: Create a Screen Recording on the Mac

1. Record a software demonstration.

   ☐ on the Camtasia Recorder, click the red **Start Recording** button

   You'll see a three-second countdown.

   ☐ before the counter gets to zero, position your mouse pointer in the center of the TextEdit window

   After the counter disappears, your every move (and the time it takes you to move) is being recorded.

   ☐ moving steadily (not too fast), move your mouse pointer to the **File** menu

   ☐ click the **Page Setup** menu item

   ☐ from the **Orientation** area, click **Landscape**

   ☐ click the **OK** button

   ☐ click the **File** menu

   ☐ click the **Page Setup** menu item

   ☐ click the **Portrait** orientation button

   ☐ click the **OK** button

2. Stop the recording process.

   ☐ press [**command**] [**option**] [**2**] on your keyboard

   Once you press the Stop recording keyboard shortcut, the recording process terminates, and a few things happen in rapid succession. First, the Camtasia Recorder application closes. Second, the Camtasia Editor opens. Third, a new project is created. The recording you created is added to the Camtasia Media Bin and inserted onto the Timeline.

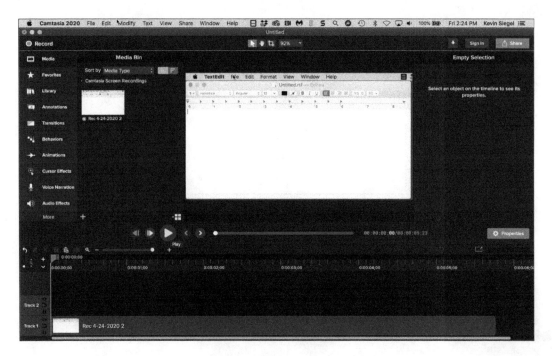

Recording Confidence Check (Mac)

1. Use the playback controls on the Camtasia Canvas to preview the recording as you learned during the last module (page 18).

2. Close the Camtasia project (there is no need to save it).

3. Record a new software demonstration of anything you'd like to record on your computer.

   For instance, use your web browser to add a Favorite, change the appearance of text in your word processor of choice, or edit the appearance of an image in your favorite image editor.

4. When finished recording, preview the recording in the Camtasia Editor.

5. Close the Camtasia project (there is no need to save it).

Notes

Module 3: Adding Media

In This Module You Will Learn About:

- Adding Videos, page 48
- Adding Images, page 52
- Multi-Track Projects, page 54
- Cursor Effects, page 58

And You Will Learn To:

- Import a Video to the Media Bin, page 48
- Add a Video to the Timeline, page 49
- Import Images, page 52
- Add a Track, page 54
- Edit Media Properties, page 57
- Add Cursor Effects, page 58

Adding Videos

During the first module of this book, you were introduced to the tools that make up Camtasia and explored the Editor interface (beginning on page 10). Then you used the Camtasia Recorder to record screen actions (beginning on page 29). Now you'll create a Camtasia project from scratch using the Camtasia Editor. The first thing you will add to your new Camtasia project is video.

Guided Activity 14: Import a Video to the Media Bin

1. Ensure that Camtasia 2020 is running.

2. On the **Welcome window**, click **New Project** or, if a Camtasia project is already open, choose **File > New Project**

3. Import a video.

   ☐ from the top left of the Editor, click **Media** to display the Media Bin

   ☐ on the **Media Bin** panel, click **Import Media**

The Open dialog box appears. Any supported video file you can access from your computer can be imported using this dialog box.

   ☐ from the **Camtasia2020Data** folder, open the **Video_Files** folder

   ☐ open/import **CreateNewFolderVideo**

The video appears in the Media Bin.

Next you'll add the media to the Timeline.

Guided Activity 15: Add a Video to the Timeline

1. Add a video to the Timeline.

   ☐ on the **Media Bin**, right-click the video and choose **Add to Timeline at Playhead**

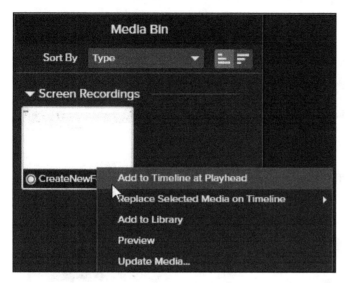

   On the Timeline, the video you added is represented by a horizontal bar.

2. Preview a project on the Canvas.

   ☐ on the **Canvas**, click the **Play** button

   The video plays just like it did via the Preview window. However, there's also an object that moves along the Timeline and it's synchronized with the preview. This object is known as the **Playhead**. You'll spend plenty of time working with the Playhead later.

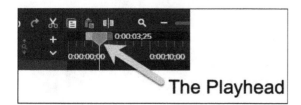

The Playhead

NOTES

3. Save the project.

    ☐ choose **File > Save**

    ☐ name the project **CreateNewFolder**, ensure you are saving to the **Camtasia2020Data**, **Projects** folder

    ☐ Mac users, ensure that **Create standalone project is selected**

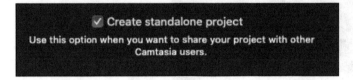

    ☐ All users: click the **Save** button

    Depending upon your platform, saved projects get a slightly different file name extension. On the PC, files get a **tscproj** extension. Mac projects get a **cmproj** extension.

    At the left, Camtasia for PC users and the tscproj extension. Projects on the Mac get a cmproj extension.

    PC users only, you'll also be alerted that to edit the project moving forward, you'll need to open the **tscproj** file with Camtasia

    ☐ PC users only, click the **OK** button

Video Confidence Check

1. Ensure that the **CreateNewFolder** project is open.

2. On the **Timeline**, right-click the video you just added and choose **Delete**.

   The video is removed from the Timeline. Now that it has been removed from the Timeline, it would no longer appear in a produced lesson. However, notice that the video remains in the Media Bin. Items in the Media Bin remain available for you to preview and add to the Timeline, but items in the Media Bin will not appear in a produced video unless they have been added to the Timeline.

3. Ensure the **Playhead** is positioned as far left of the Timeline as it will go.

4. Right-click the video in the Media Bin and choose **Add to Timeline at Playhead** to add the video to the Timeline again.

5. On the Timeline, zoom closer to the video in Track 1 by clicking the **Zoom timeline in** icon.

   The ability to Zoom closer to Timeline objects will prove useful later when you need to split the audio or synchronize the video with other Timeline objects. You can always use the **Zoom timeline out** tool to move farther away from the Timeline or drag the slider (the circle between the plus and minus signs).

6. Save the project.

Adding Images

Few things enhance an eLearning lesson better than quality images. Camtasia supports many of the standard graphic formats, including bitmaps, GIFs, and JPEGs. You can learn about the different graphic formats with a quick Internet search (one site that I find helpful is **Dan's Data** (www.dansdata.com/graphics.htm).

If you don't have access to photographs and other assets, I've had great success with BigStockPhoto.com and iStockPhoto.com. Both of these sites offer awesome collections of inexpensive, royalty-free images. You'll also find an assets Library on the TechSmith website (https://library.techsmith.com). While the TechSmith Library assets are royalty free, use of the Library requires an annual subscription.

Guided Activity 16: Import Images

1. Open an existing Camtasia project.

   ☐ choose **File > Open Project**

   ☐ from the **Camtasia2020Data > Projects** folder, open **ImageMe**

   This project is identical to the one you were just working on. It has the CreateNewFolderVideo in the Media Bin and on the Timeline.

2. Import an image to the Media Bin.

   ☐ choose **File > Import > Media**

   ☐ from the **Camtasia2020Data** folder, open the **Image_Files** folder

   ☐ select **logo.png** and then click **Open** (PC) or **Import** (Mac)

   The logo image appears in the Media Bin.

3. Import another image.

   ☐ choose **File > Import > Media**

   ☐ from the **Image_Files** folder, open/import **mainart.jpg**

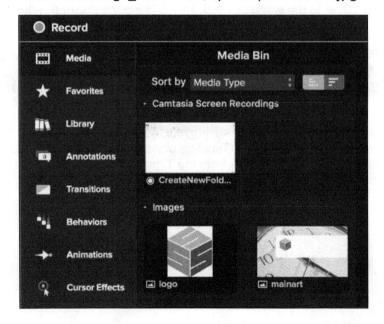

Timeline Confidence Check

1. On the **Timeline**, drag the **CreateNewFolder** video to the **right** several seconds to leave space at the left of the video for the mainart image. (You'll need at least 5 seconds of space.)

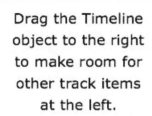

Drag the Timeline object to the right to make room for other track items at the left.

2. On the **Media Bin**, drag the **mainart** image to the beginning of Track 1 on the Timeline.

3. On the Timeline, drag the **CreateNewFolder** object **left** until it bumps up against the mainart image).

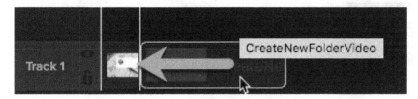

4. On the **Canvas**, click the **Play** button to preview the project.

   On the Canvas, notice that the **mainart** image appears, disappears after a few seconds, and is then replaced by the video showing how to create a new folder.

   If you want Timeline objects to appear on the Canvas one after the other, you've just learned that it's as simple as dragging (or stretching) objects left or right on the Timeline to control when they appear and how long. However, if you want multiple Timeline items on the Canvas at the same time, you'll need multiple Timeline tracks, something you'll learn about next.

5. Save your work.

NOTES

Multi-Track Projects

You've added two assets to the Timeline (the video and the mainart image). Both objects appear on a single Track called Track 1. You can easily add additional tracks to the Timeline. Once you have multiple tracks, you can precisely control when multiple objects appear on the Canvas and how items appear on the Canvas in relationship to other Timeline media. For instance, you can add your corporate logo to a new track above the video track and create a watermark effect, perfect for corporate branding.

Guided Activity 17: Add a Track

1. Ensure that the **ImageMe** project is open.

2. Insert a new track.

   ☐ on the top left of the Timeline, click **Add a track**

   On the Timeline, notice that Track 2 has been added above Track 1. Because Track 2 is above Track 1 on the Timeline, anything you add to Track 2 appears to float (stacked) above anything on Track 1 when viewed on the Canvas.

   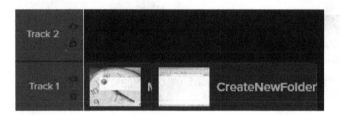

3. Add an image to the Track 2.

   ☐ move the **Playhead** to the **beginning** of the Timeline, if necessary

   ☐ on the Media Bin, right-click the **logo image** and choose **Add to Timeline at Playhead**

Only one object can be positioned on a track at a particular time on the Timeline. Because the Playhead is positioned at 0:00 time and there is an object on Track 1 at that time point, the logo is automatically added to the next available track (in this instance, the beginning of Track 2). If you hadn't manually added the second track prior to adding the image to the Timeline, the track would have been added for you.

4. Change when the logo appears on the Timeline.

   ☐ on **Track 2**, position your mouse pointer in the **middle** of the **logo**

   ☐ **drag** the logo **right** until its **left edge** lines up with the left edge of the CreateNewFolder media on Track 1

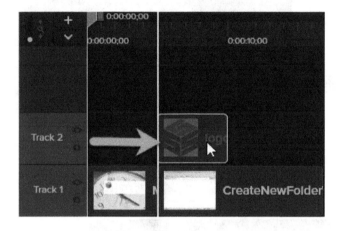

5. Position the Playhead and preview a portion of the video.

   ☐ on the **Timeline**, double-click the CreateNewFolder **video** object

   The Playhead, which indicates specific points in time and the current frame selected on the Timeline, should now be positioned just before the CreateNewFolderVideo media.

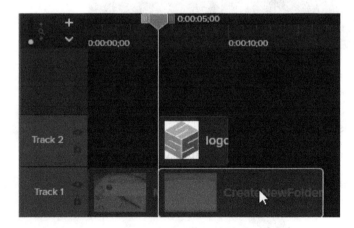

   ☐ on your keyboard, press [**spacebar**]

   On the Canvas, notice that the logo image appears in the middle of the video by default. The logo disappears after a few seconds (long before the video finishes).

6. Save your work.

NOTES

7. Extend the play time for the logo.

❑ on the Timeline, use your mouse to **point** to the **right edge** of the logo object

Note: If you are very close to the Timeline, it might be helpful to zoom out a bit before working with the Timeline objects.

❑ when your mouse pointer changes to a **double-headed arrow**, drag the **right** edge of the logo object **right** until the logo's bar ends when the video ends (as shown in the images below)

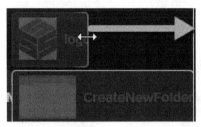 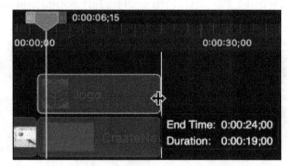

The image above is Camtasia for Windows/PC. At the right, Camtasia for the Mac. Note that the double-headed arrow used for stretching Timeline objects looks slightly different on the two operating systems.

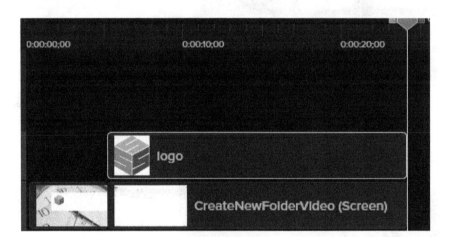

8. Preview the timing changes.

❑ on the Timeline, double-click the **CreateNewFolder** video object

On the Timeline, the Playhead should once again appear just before the **CreateNewFolder** video on the Timeline.

❑ on your keyboard, press [**spacebar**] to preview the video

On the Canvas, notice that the logo image sticks around for the duration of the video. (It's too big, and it doesn't work all that well in the middle of the video, but you'll fix those issues next.)

❑ on your keyboard, press [**spacebar**] again to stop the video preview

9. Save your work.

Guided Activity 18: Edit Media Properties

1. Ensure that the **ImageMe** project is open.

2. Display the Properties panel.

   ☐ on Track 2, right-click the **logo** and choose **Show Properties** (if you see **Hide Properties** instead, you can move to the next step)

   At the **right side** of the Editor, notice that there's a Properties panel.

3. Use the Properties panel to make the logo smaller.

   ☐ on the **Properties** panel, drag the **Scale** slider **left** to change the Scale to **50%** (if you find it difficult to get to exactly 50, type **50** into the Scale field at the right)

4. Lower the Opacity of the logo.

   ☐ on the **Properties** panel, drag the **Opacity** slider **left** to change the Opacity to **40%** (again, if you find it difficult to get to exactly 40, type **40** into the field at the right)

5. Change the logo's Canvas position.

   ☐ on the Canvas, drag the logo near the bottom right of the Canvas

6. Save your work.

Cursor Effects

Earlier in this module you added a video to the project that demonstrates the process of creating a new folder on a computer (page 48). You've previewed that video several times during this module, so it's likely that you have already noticed that in the video the mouse, through the process of creating a new folder, moves from one part of the window to the next. As the cursor moves, there are no click sounds or visual effects to draw the learner's attention to the clicks. Because the video was created with the Camtasia Recorder, the cursor can be modified in the Editor by adding such enhancements as click effects and click sounds.

> **Note:** The ability to edit the cursor in Camtasia is possible only with videos recorded by the Camtasia Recorder. Camtasia's Cursor Effects cannot be applied to software video demos created by other tools.

Guided Activity 19: Add Cursor Effects

1. Open an existing project.

   ☐ choose **File > Open Project**

   ☐ from **Camtasia2020Data > Projects**, open **MouseMe**

2. Preview the lesson.

   ☐ on the **Timeline**, double-click the **CreateNewFolder** media to move the Playhead to the beginning of the video

   ☐ on your keyboard, press [**spacebar**]

   As the video plays, pay particular attention to the mouse cursor. The more cluttered the background, the harder the cursor is to see. During the steps that follow, you'll add a visual effect to make it more noticeable.

3. Add a Highlight effect to the cursor in the video.

   ☐ on the **Timeline**, ensure that the **CreateNewFolderVideo** media is selected

   ☐ from the list of tools at the left, click **Cursor Effects**

   ☐ PC users, right-click **Cursor Highlight** and choose **Add to Selected Media**; Mac users, right-click **Highlight** and choose **Add to Selected Media**

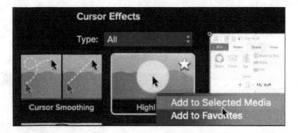

On the Timeline, the effect is added to the selected media. You can confirm video effects (and delete them) via to the **Show effects** arrow beneath the video object on the Timeline.

4. Preview the video.

   ❏ on your keyboard, press [**spacebar**]

   The cursor now sports a nifty highlight effect. *How cool is that?*

5. Change the Properties of the Cursor Effect.

   ❏ on the **Timeline**, right click the video media and choose **Show Properties**

   Note: If the menu item says **Hide Properties**, the Properties panel is already open at the right of the Camtasia window.

   ❏ on the **Properties** panel, **Cursor Highlight** area, **Color** section, select any appropriate color

   ❏ from the **Opacity** area, change the Opacity to **30%**

   ❏ from the **Size** area, drag the slider left to **30**

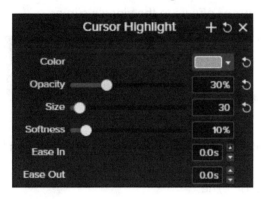

6. Preview the video.

   The cursor's Color, Size, and Opacity should reflect your changes.

Cursor Effects Confidence Check

1. On the Timeline, click **Show effects** just below the video.

2. With the effects showing, right-click the **Cursor Highlight** effect and choose **Delete** (**Remove Effect** on the Mac) to delete it.

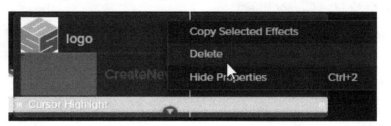

   Note: It's easy enough to accidentally delete media instead of an effect. When deleting an effect, ensure that you right-click the effect, not the video itself.

3. Spend a few moments adding different **Cursor** effects to the video's cursor.

4. Spend a few moments adding **Left Click** effects to the video's cursor.

5. PC users, save your work.
   Mac users, save and close all open projects.

6. Create a new project.

7. Import the following media from the **Camtasia2020Data > Projects > Video_Files** folder: **SmoothMyCursor**.

8. Add the **SmoothMyCursor** media to the Timeline.

9. Preview the **SmoothMyCursor** media and notice that the cursor does not move smoothly from item to item.

10. Add the following Cursor Effect to the media: **Cursor Smoothing**.

11. Preview the video.

    The cursor's path has been smoothed out nicely. However, there are delays in the cursor's movement.

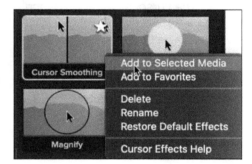

12. On the **Properties** panel, deselect **Detect Cursor Pauses**.

13. Preview the video.

    The cursor moves from point to point with fewer delays.

14. PC users: create a new project (don't save the current project when prompted).
    Mac users: close the project without saving.

iCONLOGiC
"Skills and Drills" Learning

Module 4: Groups, Annotations, Behaviors, and Transitions

In This Module You Will Learn About:

And You Will Learn To:

Groups

As you continue to add media to the Timeline, things are likely to get a bit, shall we say, frenzied. On page 54, you learned about working with multiple Timeline tracks. Moving an object in one track can easily foul up its relationship to objects on other tracks.Because object timing relationships can be complex, you'll appreciate Camtasia's ability to group objects. Rather than moving an individual object on the Timeline, and then realizing you left a related object on a different track behind, you can group objects and move multiple items at one time.

Guided Activity 20: Create a Group

1. Open **AnnotateMe** from the Camtasia2020Data Projects folder.

2. Move a Timeline object.

   ☐ on the Timeline, drag the **logo** object to the **right** by 5 or 10 seconds

   After moving the logo, notice that the CreateNewFolderVideo object does not move. Given that these two objects should appear onscreen together, it would be better to group them prior to moving either one of them.

3. Undo the last step.

   ☐ choose **Edit > Undo Move** (or press [**ctrl** or **command**] [**z**])

   The logo should now be back in its original Timeline position.

4. Create a group.

   ☐ on the Timeline, select the **CreateNewFolder** media in Track 1

   ☐ press [**shift**] and select the **logo** in Track 2 (then release [**shift**])

   Both the video and the logo should now be selected.

   ☐ right-click either of the selected objects and choose **Group**

   The selected objects are grouped. The logo, which was in Track 2, has been moved into the new group on Track 1. In the first image below, notice that the name of a group on the PC contains the word **media**; groups on the Mac contain the word **clips**. Other than this minor difference in naming conventions, grouping works the same on Mac and PCs.

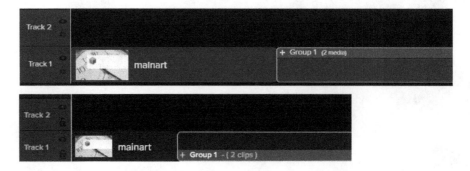

5. Name a group.

   ❑ right-click the group and choose **Rename Group**

   The group's default name, Group 1, is selected.

   ❑ change the group's name to **Creating Folders** and press [**enter**]

6. Move Timeline objects as a group.

   ❑ on the Timeline, drag the **Creating Folders** group **right** until its left edge lines up with the **30 second** mark on the Timeline

   Both objects in the group move, leaving a sizable gap between the mainart object and the group. You'll be adding media within that gap shortly.

   Note: To Ungroup objects, right-click a group and choose Ungroup (image A, below). If you'd like to see, edit, or replace grouped objects, click the plus sign in the upper left of a group to Open the group (image B). Closing a group is different on the PC and the Mac. To close a group on the PC, click the minus sign just above the open group (image C). On the Mac, an extra tab is added to the Timeline when a group is opened. Click the X on the tab to close the group (image D).

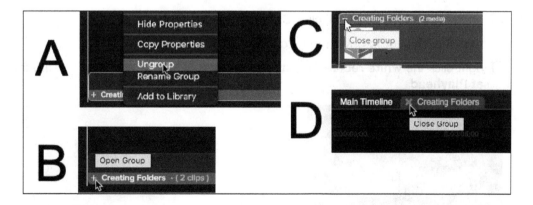

7. Remove an empty track.

   ❑ ensure that you did not Ungroup after reading the note above (if you Ungrouped an object will likely go into Track 2 and it will no longer be empty)

   ❑ at the left of the Timeline, right-click the words **Track 2** and choose **Remove Track**

   Note: Empty tracks do no harm, and it is never a requirement to remove them.

Annotations

There are several types of Annotations, including **Callouts** (shapes that can contain text), Arrows, Lines, Shapes, Motions, and Keystroke callouts. In the Demo project you opened at the beginning of this book, there are several callouts synchronized with the voiceover audio. One of the callouts from that project is shown in the image below (the words **CREATE** and **FOLDERS**). During the activities that follow, you will add and then format a few callouts.

Guided Activity 21: Add a Callout

1. Ensure that the **AnnotateMe** project is open.

2. Insert a callout.

   ☐ on the Timeline, double-click the **mainart** image to move the Playhead to the far left of the Timeline

   ☐ from the list of tools at the left, click **Annotations**

   The Annotations panel opens.

   ☐ on the **Annotations** panel, click **Callouts** (the first Annotation type)

   ☐ from the **Style** drop-down menu, choose **Basic**

   ☐ right-click the **white rectangle with the black text** and choose **Add to Timeline at Playhead**

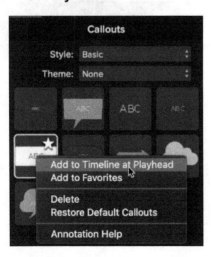

3. Remove a callout's border.

❏ with the callout selected, **Show** the **Properties** panel

❏ at the top of the **Properties** panel, click **Annotation Properties**

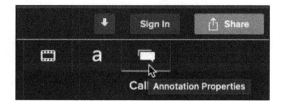

❏ on the callout Properties panel, change the **Thickness** to **0** (you can either type a **0** into the text field or drag the slider as far **left** as it will go)

4. Format the callout's text.

❏ with the callout still selected, at the top of the Properties panel, click **Text Properties**

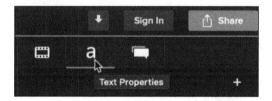

❏ change the Font to **Verdana (Regular)**

❏ change the Color to **Black**

❏ change the Size to **80**

❏ change the **Alignment** to **Left**

❏ deselect **Auto-resize text**

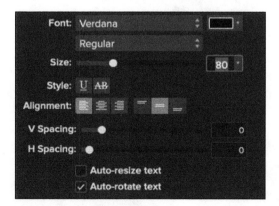

Auto-resize text, if selected, will make your text get smaller should you type more text into the text box than will fit. By deselecting Auto-resize text, you're ensuring that the font size used in this Annotation will always be 80 points.

5. Add the callout text.

☐ stretch the callout so that is about as wide as the white area within the mainart image

☐ replace the existing text in the callout with the words **CREATE FOLDERS**

☐ resize and position the callout on the Canvas similar to the image below

6. Save your work.

Themes

When adding Annotations to the Timeline, it's a good bet that you'll want the appearance of the new objects to be consistent across the entire project. Similar to Object Styles in other development tools and Word processors you've likely used previously, Themes can contain formatting options as object colors and fonts. Once you've created a Theme, you can quickly apply them to selected Timeline objects.

Guided Activity 22: Create and Apply a Theme

1. Ensure that the **AnnotateMe** project is open.

2. Add a second callout to the Timeline.

   ☐ on the **Timeline**, double-click the **mainart** image to move the Playhead to the **far left** of the Timeline

   ☐ from the **Annotations** tools, click **Callouts**

   ☐ from the **Style** drop-down menu, choose **Basic**

   ☐ right-click the **white rectangle with the black text** and choose **Add to Timeline at Playhead**

   The new callout is using default formatting and does not match the appearance of your first callout.

3. Apply a Theme to an object.

   ☐ with the newest callout selected on the Canvas, click either **Text** or **Annotation** on the **Properties** panel

   ☐ from the **Themes** drop-down menu, choose **Default**

The font formatting and background color of the selected callout change to reflect the properties of the Default Theme.

4. Create a new Theme.

☐ with the newest callout selected, click the **Theme** drop-down menu and choose **Manage Themes**

The **Theme Manager** opens.

☐ click the **plus sign** and choose **New Theme**

The **Create Theme** dialog box opens.

☐ name the new Theme **SSS Theme**

☐ click the **OK** button

Your new theme is now ready for editing.

5. Set a Theme's Font.

☐ from within the **Theme Manager**, and with the **SSS Theme** selected, click the **Fonts** tab

☐ change **Font 1** to **Verdana**

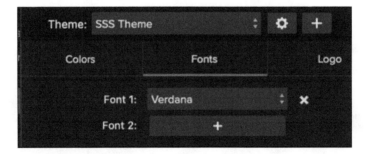

6. Set a Theme's Colors.

    ☐ from within the **Theme Manager**, and with the **SSS Theme** selected, click the **Colors** tab

    ☐ change the **Foreground** color to **Black** (this controls the color of the text in the callout)

    ☐ change the **Background1** color to **White**

    ☐ if necessary, change the **Annotation Background** to **Background1**

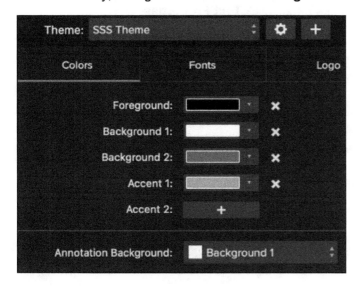

    ☐ click the **Save** button

7. Apply Themes to multiple callouts.

    ☐ select both of the callouts you've added so far (selecting one and [**shift**]-**clicking** the second one works great)

    ☐ from the **Themes** drop-down menu on the **Properties** panel, choose **Default**

    Both callouts take on the attributes of the Default Theme.

    ☐ with both callouts selected, choose **SSS Theme** from the **Themes** drop-down menu

    Both callouts take on the attributes of the SSS Theme you created. If you've created object styles in other programs, then this behavior will be familiar to you. Camtasia Themes are a bit limited. You cannot currently control most of an object's Properties with a Theme (such as border thickness, color, drop shadows, and more). I'm hopeful that as Camtasia continues to be updated by TechSmith, more and more formatting power will be added to the Themes feature.

8. Delete just the second callout you added.

Guided Activity 23: Apply Image Color to Callout Text

1. Ensure that the **AnnotateMe** project is open.

2. In the callout, highlight the word **CREATE**.

3. Pick up color from an image and apply it to selected text.

   ☐ at the top of the **Properties** panel, click **Text Properties**

   ☐ from the **Choose any color** drop-down menu, select **Select color from image**

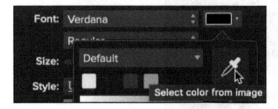

   ☐ using the **Select color from image** tool, click the green "S" on the logo

   The logo color you clicked with the **Select color from image** tool is applied to the highlighted text in the callout.

4. Save your work.

Callouts Confidence Check

1. Click in front of the word **FOLDERS** and press [**enter**].

2. Press [spacebar] a few times to indent the word **FOLDERS**.

3. On the Timeline, right-click the callout and **Copy** it to the clipboard.

4. On the Timeline, position the **Playhead** just to the **right** of the callout.

5. PC users, right-click the existing callout and choose **Paste**.
   Mac users, right-click just to the right of the callout and choose **Paste Media at Playhead**

6. Drag the newest callout so it is positioned just after the first callout in Track 2.

Track 2	CREATE FOLDERS	Callou	CREATE FOLDERS	Callou
Track 1	maina			

7. Double-click the new callout and change the word **CREATE** to **RENAME**.

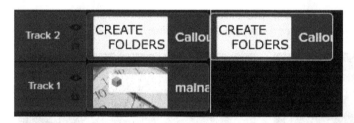

8. On the Timeline, position the Playhead just to the right of the second callout.

9. PC users, right-click the existing callout and choose **Paste**.
   Mac users, right-click just to the right of the callout and choose **Paste Media at Playhead**

10. Drag the newest callout so it is positioned just after the second callout in Track 2.

11. Drag the new callout up against the second callout.

12. Double-click the new callout and change the word **CREATE** to **DELETE**.

13. Change the word **FOLDERS** to **RESTORE**.

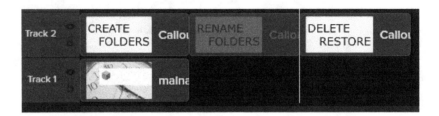

14. Save your work.

15. Create a **new** Camtasia project.

16. Spend a few moments adding some of the other Annotations to the project. (There is no need to save the new project so play as much as you'd like.)

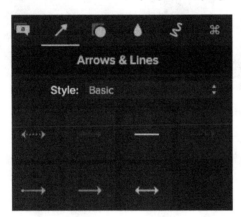

As you add the Annotations, notice the formatting options available to you on the Properties panel. You'll find that the options vary depending upon the type of Annotation you're working with.

17. Select any annotation and notice that there is a star icon.

18. Click the star icon to turn it yellow and add the object as a **Favorite**.

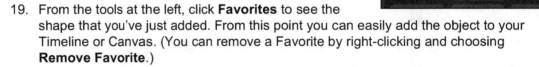

19. From the tools at the left, click **Favorites** to see the shape that you've just added. From this point you can easily add the object to your Timeline or Canvas. (You can remove a Favorite by right-clicking and choosing **Remove Favorite**.)

20. PC users, create a new project (there is no need to save the existing project). Mac users, close all open projects (there is no need to save anything).

Note: Favorites added to one project will be available to all projects.

Behaviors

Behaviors, also known as Effects, are animations that are typically used to add some visual excitement to your project. Behaviors can be attached to images, video clips, and several types of Annotations. A Behavior can be added to a single object or stacked together with other Behaviors to create unique effects.

Guided Activity 24: Add a Behavior to a Callout

1. Open **BehaveMe** from the Camtasia2020Data Projects folder.

   This project has several callouts that have been added to Tracks 2 and 3. In particular, notice the three ampersands (**&**) added to Track 2 at **10;05**, **15;18**, and **20;18**.

   The stacking order of assets on the Timeline is important. Notice that each ampersand is **behind** the callouts you added earlier. The stacking effect was easily attained by placing the ampersand in a lower Timeline track.

   In the image above, the **DELETE RESTORE** callout is in Track 3; the ampersand is in Track 2. Objects in higher tracks are positioned above objects in lower tracks. In the next step, you'll be adding a Behavior to the ampersands.

2. Add a Behavior to a callout.

   ☐ on Track 2, double-click the first **ampersand** positioned at **10;05** on the Timeline to highlight object on both the Timeline and on the Canvas

   ☐ from the list of tools at the left, click **Behaviors**

   ☐ right-click **Jump And Fall** and choose **Add to Selected Media**

NOTES

The Jump and Fall effect is added to the callout and appears below the Timeline object in an Effects area. Any effect can be removed from an object by showing the effects, right-clicking an effect, and then choosing **Delete** (PC) or **Remove Effect** (Mac).

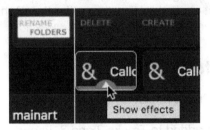

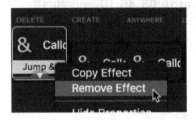

3. Preview the effect.

    ☐ on the Timeline, move the **Playhead** just to the left of the **ampersand** you just altered

    ☐ press [**spacebar**] on your keyboard **or** click the **Play** button on the Canvas

    When the Playhead gets to **DELETE RESTORE** callout, the ampersand drops in from the top of the Canvas, bounces a few times, and then drops off the bottom of the Canvas. Next you'll delay the appearance of the ampersand to enhance the effect.

4. Use the Timeline to delay the appearance of an object on the Canvas.

    ☐ on the **Timeline**, drag the **left edge** of the **ampersand** callout **right** a few seconds

5. Preview the timing change.

    ☐ on the Timeline, move the **Playhead** just to the left of the **RENAME FOLDERS** callout (the second callout on Track 2)

    ☐ press [**spacebar**] on your keyboard **or** click the **Play** button on the Canvas

    A few seconds after the **DELETE RESTORE** callout appears on the Canvas, the animated ampersand appears and does its thing.

6. Modify the Properties of a Behavior.

    ☐ on Track 2, double-click the **ampersand** you've been working with to highlight it on the Canvas (the first ampersand)

    Currently, the ampersand drops in from the top of the Canvas. Let's see what other tricks you can make the callout perform.

❑ on the **Properties** panel, select **Behavior Properties**

The Jump & Fall effect has three tabs: **In**, **During**, and **Out**. The **In** tab allows you to control what the Effect does when the object first makes an appearance on the Canvas. The **During** tab controls what the object does while it's on the Canvas. The **Out** tab lets you control what the effect does when the object leaves the Canvas.

❑ from the **Jump & Fall** Properties area, select the **In** tab

❑ from the **Style** drop-down menu, choose **Hinge**

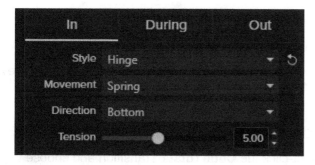

Behaviors Confidence Check

1. With the Playhead positioned just to the left of the **ampersand** you just altered, preview the effect on the Canvas.

   The ampersand should swing up from the bottom of the Canvas.

2. Spend a few moments playing with the **In**, **During**, and **Out** settings available on the **Properties** panel.

3. Add a Behavior to the remaining two ampersands (the ampersands are positioned on the Timeline at **15;18**, and **20;18**).

4. Preview the effects and adjust the timing of the ampersand callouts as you see fit.

5. Adjust the **In**, **During**, and **Out** properties of the effects as you see fit.

6. Select and then group mainart image and the callouts (name the group **Introduction to folders**).

7. Save your work. (Mac users, close the project.)

Transitions

You can use Transitions to add a smooth, professional visual break between clips in a project. There are several Transition types available on the Transitions panel, including Glow, Fold, and, my personal favorite, Cube rotate.

Guided Activity 25: Add a Transition to a Group

1. Open **TransitionMe** from the **Camtasia2020Data** > **Projects** folder.

2. Preview a few Transitions.

    ❑ from the tools at the left, click **Transitions**

    ❑ from the list of **Transitions**, hover above **Fade**

    A sample of the Fade Transition appears on the thumbnail.

    ❑ on the **Transitions** panel, hover above the **Wheel** Transition to see a preview

    ❑ on the **Transitions** panel, hover above the **Cube rotate** Transition to see a preview

3. Add a Transition to selected media.

    ❑ on the **Timeline**, select the **Get Ready** group

    ❑ on the **Transitions** panel, right-click the **Cube rotate** Transition and choose **Add to Selected Media**

On the Timeline, the Cube Rotate transition has been added to the beginning of the selected group, and it's been added to the beginning of the next group. You can tell that a transition has been added via the green rectangles. The transition was added to the second group (even though you didn't select that group) because, by default, transitions are added to the beginning and end of a selected group and to the beginning of the next group that it is touching.

4. Save your work.

Guided Activity 26: Modify Transition Timing

1. Ensure that the **TransitionMe** project is open.

2. Preview the project from the beginning.

   As the video plays on the Canvas, the Cube rotate transition appears at the beginning and end of the first clip and again at the beginning of the second clip. It's a cool effect, but you'd like to speed it up a bit.

3. Modify Transition Timing.

   ☐ on the Timeline, drag the **right edge** of the first green transition icon a bit to the **left**

   ☐ drag the **left** edge second green transition a bit to the **right**

4. Preview the project from the beginning.

   The timing for each transition should be a bit faster than before.

Transitions Confidence Check

1. Working in the **TransitionMe** project, add any Transition(s) you like to each of the groups.

2. Preview the project to see the transitions.

3. Save your work.

Notes

iCONLOGiC

"Skills and Drills" Learning

Module 5: Audio

In This Module You Will Learn About:

- Music Tracks, page 80
- Voice Narration, page 85
- Splitting Media, page 89
- Audio Editing, page 91

And You Will Learn To:

- Add Music From the Library, page 80
- Fade Audio, page 83
- Record Voice Narration, page 86
- Split a Music Clip, page 89
- Rename Tracks, page 91
- Silence, Delete, and Ripple Delete, page 92

Music Tracks

There are multiple sources for music that can be added to a Camtasia project. Some of the more popular free sources are the Music Tracks folder within the Camtasia Library, the TechSmith Camtasia audio assets at https://library.techsmith.com/camtasia, or music tracks you may already have on your computer.

According to TechSmith, you can use their media assets royalty free. When something from a trusted source is labeled royalty free, it means you can confidently use those assets without the need to pay fees to the copyright holder. However, prior to using assets obtained from any other source besides TechSmith, you should ensure you have documented permission to use those assets from the appropriate copyright holder.

Guided Activity 27: Add Music From the Library

1. Open **AudioMe** from the Camtasia2020Data Projects folder.

2. Add background music to the project from the Library.

   ☐ from the list of tools at the left, click **Library**

   ☐ from the **Library** drop-down menu, ensure that **Camtasia 2020** is selected

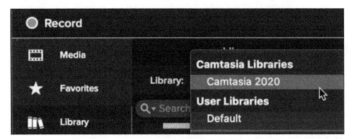

   ☐ double-click the **Music Tracks** folder to open it

   ☐ ensure the **Playhead** is positioned at the **beginning** of the **Timeline**

   ☐ from the **Music Tracks** folder, right-click any of the music files and choose **Add to Timeline at Playhead**

The audio file appears on the Timeline in Track 2 as a series of sharp lines—a waveform.

3. Preview the first part of the video to hear the background music.

Library Audio Confidence Check

1. On the Timeline select and delete the background music you just added from the Library.

2. On the Media Bin, notice that although you've removed the music from the Timeline, a copy of the unused media asset is retained.

3. From the Library, add a different Music Track to the Timeline.

4. Preview the video to hear the newly added music.

5. On the Timeline select and delete the new background music.

6. On the Media Bin, notice that the newest music is still referenced even though it is no longer being used on the Timeline.

7. Right-click the Media Bin and choose **Delete Unused Media**.

Note: Deleting Unused Media isn't a requirement but does keep the bin clutter-free.

8. Save your work.

Guided Activity 28: Import Music

1. Ensure that the **AudioMe** project is open.

2. Import an audio file to the Media Bin.

   ☐ choose **File > Import > Media**

   ☐ navigate to **Camtasia2020Data > Audio_Files**

   ☐ from the **Audio_Files** folder, open/import **2Step1.mp3**

   The imported audio clip appears in the Media Bin.

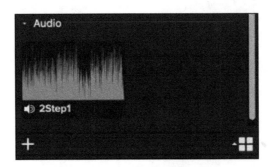

3. Add the imported audio to the Timeline.

   ☐ ensure the **Playhead** is positioned at the **beginning** of the **Timeline**

   ☐ on the **Media Bin**, right-click **2Step1.mp3** and choose **Add to Timeline at Playhead**

4. Preview the video to hear the background audio you just added to the Timeline.

   If you listen to the music until the end, you'll notice that the audio fades out nicely. However, if you preview the beginning of the video, you'll notice that the audio starts just a bit too abruptly. You will take care of that next when you learn how to fade music in (or out).

Guided Activity 29: Fade Audio

1. Ensure that the **AudioMe** project is open.

2. Fade audio in.

   ☐ on the **Timeline**, select the background music on **Track 2**

   ☐ from the tools at the left, click **Audio Effects**

   ☐ from the **Audio Effects** panel, right-click **Fade In** and choose **Add to Selected Media**

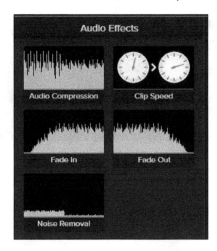
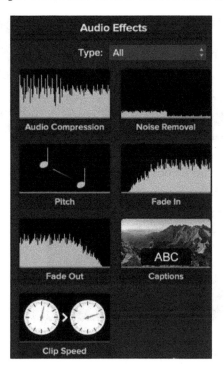

Shown above, the Audio Effects for Camtasia 2020 for Windows; at the right, the Mac version of Camtasia 2020.

Notice that a ramp has been added to the left of the waveform.

The ramp begins at the bottom of the waveform and then gets taller until the audio hits a consistent level. You can manually drag the green line to control how the audio fades in, but you'll probably be happy with the level established automatically by Camtasia.

3. Preview the beginning of the video to hear the audio fade effect.

4. If you'd like the fade effect to last a bit longer, drag the green circle on the waveform **right** to extend the fade timing.

Fading Confidence Check

1. Delete the background music from the Timeline.

2. Using the Library, add any Music Track to the Timeline.

   The music that you just added to the Timeline plays far longer than your other Timeline assets.

3. Drag the **right side** of the background music **left** until the end of the music lines up with the assets in the last group on the Timeline.

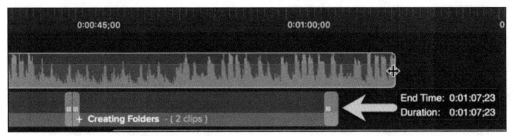

4. Use the **Audio Effects** to add **Fade In** and **Fade Out** effects to the music on the Timeline as you see fit.

5. Preview the video to hear the fade effects.

6. Save your work. (Mac users: You can close the project.)

Voice Narration

Camtasia allows you to record your voice and sound effects and add them to the Timeline. If you plan to record audio, consider the following:

Voiceover Scripts: You saw an example of an eLearning script on page 22. It's a good idea to rehearse the voiceover script before recording the audio in Camtasia. Rehearsals are the perfect opportunity to find any areas of the script that are going to cause you trouble while recording.

Location, Location, Location: You might be surprised by how much noise there is in an average office or home. Is there a nearby faucet dripping? Is the overhead fan making noise? Is your neighbor or family member coughing or sneezing? It's possible you're creating your eLearning at home where you're sure it's quieter. But is the dog barking? Are the kids playing just outside your door? While you have become adept at tuning out everyday sounds, your microphone hears—and records—everything. Before using your office or cubicle as a recording studio, stop and listen to what's happening around you, and try to get your surroundings as quiet as possible.

Microphones vs. Headsets: A microphone is what you'll use to record your audio. It can be positioned on your desk, on a stand, suspended from the ceiling, or attached to your clothing. Typical headsets combine a microphone, typically a boom that can be adjusted up and down and further or closer to your mouth, and a listening device. As the name implies, a headset is usually positioned on your head. You can use either a microphone or a headset when you record audio. If you'd like to see and hear a side-by-side comparison of several recording devices, **Rick Zanotti** is an excellent resource. Visit **youtube.com** and search for "**eLearnChat Microphones for eLearning**" for an entire video series Rick created that covers everything from Sennheiser to Shure to Neumann to Blue Bird.

Microphone Placement: The microphone should be positioned approximately six inches from your mouth to reduce the chance that nearby sounds will be recorded. Ideally, you should position the microphone above your nose and pointed down at your mouth. Also, if you position the microphone just to the side of your mouth, you can soften the sound of the letters S and P.

Microphone Technique: It's a good idea to keep a glass of water close and, just before recording, take a drink. To eliminate breathing and lip-smack sounds, turn away from the microphone, take a deep breath, exhale, take another deep breath, open your mouth, turn back toward the microphone, and start speaking. Speak slowly. When recording for the first time, many people race through the content. *Take your time.*

Monitor Your Audio Level As You Record: When recording your audio, you will see an Input Level meter on Camtasia's Voice Narration panel indicating how well the recording process is going. When the meter is green to yellow, you're fine. However, when the meter is orange to red, you are being warned that you are too close to the microphone or that you are speaking too loudly.

Guided Activity 30: Record Voice Narration

1. Using a word processor, open **CreatingFoldersVoiceoverScript** from **Camtasia2020Data > Other_Assets**.

   Let's pretend for a moment that you've been hired to serve as the voiceover talent for an eLearning project. It's quite possible you'd get a script similar to the file you've just opened.

   > **Audio File 1:**
   > Welcome to Super Simplistic Solutions learning series.
   > This is lesson one: Creating New Folders.
   >
   > **Audio File 2:**
   > This lesson is going to teach you how to create a new folder on your computer, how to rename it, and how to both delete and restore recycled items.
   >
   > **Audio File 3:**
   > When creating folders keep in mind that you can create as many folders as you need.

2. Rehearse the audio script.

   ☐ using a measured (not too fast nor too slow) cadence, read the following out loud:

   Welcome to Super Simplistic Solutions learning series.

   This is lesson one: Creating New Folders.

   Next you'll record your voice in Camtasia. You can close the script now if you'd like.

3. Using Camtasia, open **NarrateMe** from the Camtasia2020Data Projects folder.

4. Record voiceover audio.

   ☐ on the **Timeline**, position the Playhead on the **Lesson 1** group

   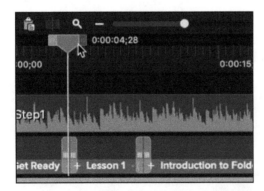

   ☐ from the tools at the left, click **Voice Narration**

On the Voice Narration panel, notice that I have already pasted the part of the voiceover script you'll be recording. Alternatively, you could print the script and have it beside you during the recording phase.

❏ if necessary, select **your microphone** from the drop-down menu at the top of the Voice Narration panel

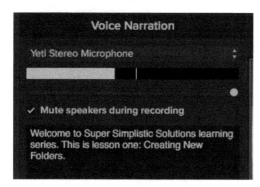

❏ ensure **Mute timeline during recording** is selected

Muting the Timeline is a good idea for this video because you have background audio in Track 2. If you don't mute the audio, the music could play through your computer speakers and ruin your voiceover audio.

And now, prepare yourself! Once you start the recording process, there isn't a count-down or any kind of warning. Instead, Camtasia simply starts recording. While you are recording, the video will play on the Canvas so you can see what's happening in your lesson while you narrate.

❏ click the **Start Voice Recording** button

There's a difference between the Mac and PC when it comes to recording audio. In the image above at the left, the Start Voice Recording button for PC users does not have a microphone icon. When finished recording audio on the PC, you are prompted to give the audio file a name. On the Mac, recorded audio is automatically saved and the media added to the Timeline.

❏ using a slow, deliberate cadence, read the following out loud:

Welcome to Super Simplistic Solutions learning series.

This is lesson one: Creating New Folders.

5. When finished, click the **Stop** button.

   PC users, the Save Narration As dialog box opens.
   Mac users, the audio is automatically saved and added to the Timeline.

6. PC users only: Name the file **My_Lesson1_Voiceover** and save it to the **Audio_Files** folder within the **Camtasia2020Data** folder.

NOTES

All users, your voiceover narration appears on a new track on the Timeline. In addition, the new audio has been added to the Media Bin.

7. Preview the video.

   You should be able to hear your new voiceover audio. However, notice that the audio is hard to hear because the background music is playing at the same time. You'll fix that shortly.

8. Save your work. (Mac users: You can close the project.)

Splitting Media

You will find Camtasia's ability to split media segments on the Timeline to be a valuable feature. Have you imported an audio clip that's too long and difficult to manage? Click at the top of Timeline where you want to split the audio clip and quickly split the clip into as many segments as you need. Want to add a transition in the middle of a video clip? Because transitions cannot be inserted in the middle of a clip, click where you need a transition and insert a split.

Guided Activity 31: Split a Music Clip

1. Open **SplitMe** from the Camtasia2020Data Projects folder.

    This is basically the same project you were just working on except the voiceover audio that you recorded and inserted during the last activity has been replaced by a file named audio_file01.

2. Preview the video and notice, as mentioned at the end of the last activity, the background music and voiceover audio are playing at the same time, making it difficult to understand what the narrator is saying.

3. Lock Tracks.

    ❏ at the far left of the Timeline, click the padlock icon to the left of **Track 1** and **Track 3** to **lock** those tracks (only **Track 2** should remain unlocked)

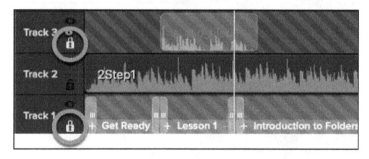

You are about to split the background music into two parts and then manipulate the two audio pieces on the Timeline so that they don't fight with the voiceover audio. During the splitting process, it's possible not only to split the background music but also to inadvertently split media in other tracks. Now that you have locked two of the three tracks, only the media in Track 2 (which is unlocked) will be affected.

4. Split the background music in Track 2 into two segments.

    ❏ on the top of the Timeline, click at the **4;29** mark to position the Playhead

    ❏ on the **Timeline**, select the media in **Track 2**

    ❏ right-click the **Playhead** and choose **Split Selected**

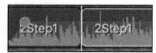

Audio Timing Confidence Check

1. Select the second (larger) segment of the background music.

2. Drag the **left edge** of the segment to the **right** until it lines up with the end of the **audio_file01** media in **Track 3**.

3. Select the **first segment of the background music** and, using the **Audio Effects** panel, **Fade Out** the media.

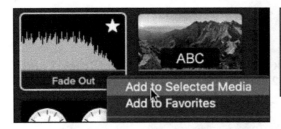

4. Select the second segment of the background music and **Fade In** the media.

5. Preview the video.

   The background music stops pretty much when the narrator begins to speak. Nice. The music does not start again until *after* the narrator is finished speaking.

   There's a problem now with the timing for Lesson 1 group. The group isn't on the Canvas quite long enough to match the voiceover audio. To fix that, you'll need to change the timing of a few Timeline objects.

6. Save your work. (Mac users: You can close the project.)

Audio Editing

Earlier in this module you learned how to edit an audio clip by fading the volume in and out. Camtasia offers you other editing options, such as the ability to cut segments of a waveform and even to replace unwanted audio with silence.

Guided Activity 32: Rename Tracks

1. Open **EditMyAudio** from the **Camtasia2020Data** Projects folder.

   This project is similar to the project you were just working on with a few notable exceptions. First, all of the tracks are unlocked. Second, two of the tracks, Voiceover and Background Audio, have names that are more descriptive than the default names Track 1, Track 2, etc.

   There's also additional voiceover audio in the Voiceover track.

2. Rename a track.

   ☐ on the far left of the Timeline, double-click the name **Track 1**

   ☐ replace the text with the word **Main** and press [**enter**]

   While naming Timeline tracks is optional. I find it's a helpful step especially when dealing with larger projects that contain more than a few tracks.

NOTES

Guided Activity 33: Silence, Delete, and Ripple Delete

1. Ensure that the **EditMyAudio** project is open.

2. Preview an audio clip.

    ☐ on the **Media Bin**, double-click **audio_file02_silence** to preview the media

   There are two strange sounds in the clip, and there's a bit of dead air at the end of the audio file. You have two choices for removing unwanted audio segments: delete the content or replace the content with **Silence**. When you delete the content, the media's duration is reduced by the amount of audio that is deleted. However, if your goal is to simply remove a problem in the audio clip (such as click sounds) without altering the duration of the media, using Silence is an ideal solution.

3. Close the media's Preview window.

4. Lock both the **Background** and **Main** tracks.

   As you learned earlier, locking a track ensures changes made to other unlocked tracks will not affect locked tracks.

5. Replace a selection of audio with Silence.

    ☐ on the **Voiceover** track, double-click **audio_file02_silence** to position the Playhead at the beginning of the audio file

    ☐ at the top of the **Timeline**, drag the **Zoom** slider right to zoom much closer to the Timeline

   At this enhanced view, you can get a better look at the waveform that makes up the audio file. You can see that the narrator's audio levels are consistent across the wave.

Take a look at about the **15 second** mark on the Timeline. There's a spike in the wave that isn't consistent with the rest of the wave. This part of the wave is an erroneous sound that you need to edit.

☐ position the Playhead to the beginning of the errant sound

☐ drag the Playhead's red out point right to highlight the sound

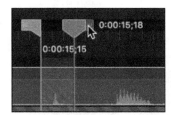

☐ right-click the selection and choose **Silence Audio**

The errant sound is removed without altering the playtime of the media.

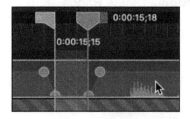

6. On the Timeline, double-click the Playhead.

   The red box at the right of the Playhead snaps back to the Playhead.

7. Delete selected media.

☐ on the Timeline, scroll **right** to the end of the **audio_file02_silence** media

There is a bit of dead air in the audio_file02_silence media that you can delete.

☐ on the Timeline, position the Playhead at **19;21** (this is the point in the media where the narrator is finished speaking and there's dead air)

☐ drag the Playhead's red out point **right** to select through the end of the **audio_file02_silence** media

☐ right-click the selection and choose **Delete** (PC) or **Delete Range** (Mac)

The selected portion of the audio clip is removed **leaving a gap** on the Timeline. You can delete both the content and the gap by using Ripple Delete instead of Delete.

8. Undo the last step.

9. Ripple Delete selected media.

☐ ensure that the dead air is still selected in the Voiceover track

☐ PC users, right-click the selection and choose **Ripple Delete**
Mac users, right-click the selection and choose **Ripple Delete Range**

The gap to the right of the deleted content is filled automatically by content to the right of the selection.

Audio Editing Confidence Check

1. There's another errant sound at about the 16-second mark on the Timeline.

2. Select and then replace the sound with Silence.

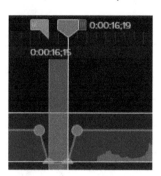

Note: Remember to double-click the Playhead to return it to its default setting (the red box should snap back to the Playhead).

3. Save your work. (Mac users: You can close the project.)

Notes

iCONLOGiC
"Skills and Drills" Learning

Module 6: Sharing

In This Module You Will Learn About:

- Standalone Videos and Web Output, page 98

And You Will Learn To:

- Export a Video on the Mac, page 98
- Export a Mac Project as a Web Page, page 101
- Create a Standalone Video on the PC, page 103
- Create a Web Video on the PC, page 106
- Add a Watermark to PC Projects, page 108
- Share to YouTube, page 111

Standalone Videos and Web Output

As you have worked through the first several modules in this book, you learned how to record a video using the Recorder (page 30). Then, beginning on page 48, you learned how to add video to the Editor. Then you added images (page 52), Annotations (page 64), Behaviors (page 73), and audio (page 79).

At some point you are going to want to wrap up the development process and Share (otherwise known as rendering) your project into a format that your learners can use. Keep in mind that to use your Shared content, learners will not need TechSmith Camtasia. Assuming learners have access to your Shared content, they can use free resources, such as web browsers or media players, that are already installed on their computer by default.

Camtasia's Share menu contains several menu items that allow you to quickly render your finished project. For instance, you can Share a standalone video that you can email to a learner or upload to a corporate server. The standalone video can be opened by free video players, such as Media Player for the PC or QuickTime on the Mac.

You can Share your project as a Web page so it can be viewed with a web browser or a zipped content package for use within a Learning Management System (LMS).

Shared content can be used by learners on devices such as desktop computers, laptops, and mobile devices (smart-phones, tablets, etc.). There are even options allowing you to Share directly to media servers like Screencast.com, YouTube, Vimeo, or Google Drive.

During the next few activities you'll learn how to share your project as a standalone video and as a Web Page. The process of Sharing is very different for Mac and PC users. First up, Mac users. PC users can skip ahead to page 103.

Guided Activity 34: Export a Video on the Mac

1. Open **ShareMe** from the Camtasia2020Data Projects folder.

2. Produce the video for the web.

   ☐ choose **Share > Local File**

   The Export As dialog box opens.

   ☐ change the **Export As** name to **Create_Folders_MP4_Only**

   ☐ navigate to the **Camtasia2020Data > Produced_Videos** folder

   ☐ from the **File format** drop-down menu at the bottom of the dialog box, choose **Export to MP4 (.mp4)**

   ☐ click the **Export** button

The project exports. You can track the rendering progress via the dialog box shown below. While your project is rendering, you won't be able to work within Camtasia without first canceling the export process.

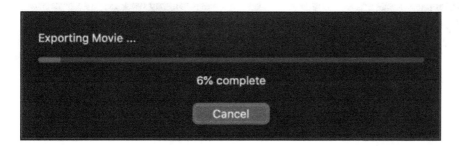

Once the export is complete, you'll see an **Export finished** dialog box.

☐ click the **Reveal in Finder** button

The Produced Videos folder opens. The only file in the folder at this point is the single video that you just exported.

3. Open the video file in a media player.

☐ right-click (or [**control**] click) the video and choose **Open With > QuickTime Player.app**

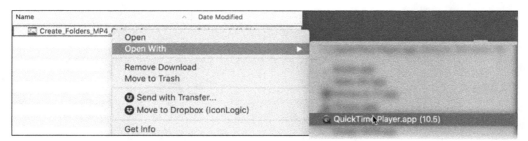

The published video opens.

☐ click the **Play** button on the playbar to start the video

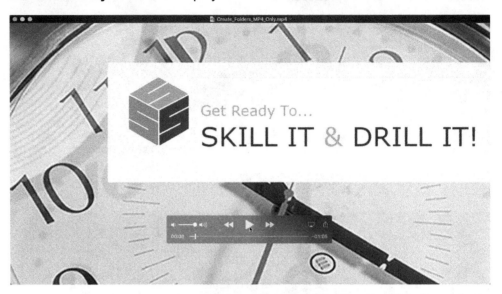

I don't know about you, but I think this whole production process went just a bit too smoothly. I bet you're thinking that I set this project up in advance so that when you produced it things would go perfectly. And I'm betting that you're betting that once you try to do this on your own, the wheel's going to come off the cart and nothing is going to work as smoothly as it just did.

Let me assure you that the production process you just worked through was based on default settings you'll find in Camtasia "out of the box." There was nothing in the ShareMe video set up in advance to ensure success in the Sharing process. In fact, you can run through the production process using any Camtasia project, and your result should be the same as those shown in this activity.

You will get a chance to play with some of the other Sharing options in a bit. For now, enjoy your progress. Believe it or not, you are now a published eLearning author. Congratulations!

4. Close the media player and return to the Camtasia project.

Guided Activity 35: Export a Mac Project as a Web Page

1. Ensure that the **ShareMe** project is open.

2. Export the project as a Web Page.

   ☐ choose **Share > Local File**

   ☐ change the **Export as** name to **ShareMe_Web_Version**

   ☐ if necessary, navigate to the **Camtasia2020Data > Produced_Videos** folder

   ☐ from the **File format** drop-down menu at the bottom of the dialog box, choose **Export to MP4 (.mp4)**

   ☐ select **Export as Web Page**

   ☐ click the **Export** button

   ☐ once the Export process is complete, click the **Reveal in Finder** button

   The last time you shared the project, you exported the project as a video. And once the video was exported, the process yielded a single file. This time, you've created a website with assets that rely on each other to correctly work in a browser. When you upload these assets to a web server, the assets must be kept together.

   ☐ open the **ShareMe_Web_Version** folder

   There's single html file in the folder (this is the start page for the lesson) and a media folder containing several required assets.

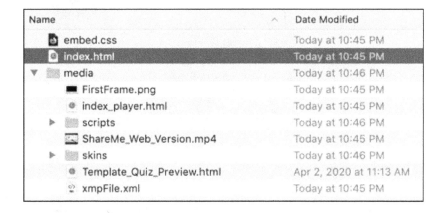

3. View the exported project in a web browser.

    ❏ from within the **ShareMe_Web_Version** folder, double-click **index.html**

    The rendered project opens in your default web browser.

    ❏ click the **Play** button in the middle of the screen to play the lesson

4. When finished, close the browser window.

5. Return to the Camtasia project.

    The next few activities are for PC users only. Mac users, skip ahead to the "Share to YouTube" activity on page 111.

Guided Activity 36: Create a Standalone Video on the PC

1. Open **ShareMe** from the Camtasia2020Data Projects folder.

2. Share the project as a video.

   ☐ choose **Share > Local File**

   The Production Wizard opens.

   ☐ choose **MP4 only (up to 720p)** from the drop-down menu

   Because the Canvas Dimensions for this project is 1280x720, selecting **up to 720** is an appropriate choice. (**Note:** You can check and change the size of the Canvas by choosing **File > Project Settings**.)

   ☐ click the **Next** button

   The **Where would you like to save your video files(s)?** screen appears.

3. Select a file name and folder.

   ☐ change the **Production name** to **ShareMe_MP4_Only**

   ☐ click the **yellow folder** at the right of the **Folder** drop-down menu

   ☐ from the **Camtasia2020Data** folder, open the **Produced_Videos** folder

   ☐ click the **Save** button

   You should be back in the **Where would you like to save your video files(s)?** window.

   ☐ ensure the remaining options match the picture below

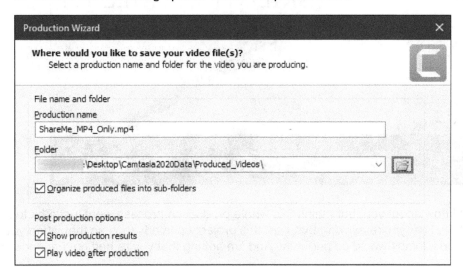

NOTES

By selecting **Organize produced files into sub-folders**, you ensure that the rendered video and its support files are kept together. The video you just rendered is a standalone video and does not require support files. Nevertheless, other formats that you produce will require several support files.

The two **Post production options**, which you also left selected, show a report of the production process in case there were errors and ensure that your rendered video plays automatically once the rendering process is complete.

4. Render the video.

   ☐ click the **Finish** button

   You can track the process on the Rendering Project screen. Generally speaking, the longer your video and the more audio clips you used on the Timeline, the longer the rendering process takes to complete.

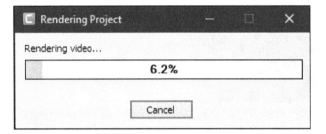

Once the rendering process is complete, the video automatically opens in your default video player and begins to play.

I don't know about you, but I think this whole production process went just a bit too smoothly. I bet you're thinking that I set this project up in advance so that when you produced it things would go perfectly. And I'm betting that you're betting that once you try to do this on your own, the wheel's going to come off the cart, and nothing is going to work as smoothly as it just did.

Let me assure you that the production process you just worked through was based on default settings you'll find in Camtasia "out of the box." There was nothing in the ShareMe video set up in advance to ensure success in the production process. In fact, you can run through the production process using any Camtasia project, and your result should match those shown in this activity.

You will get a chance to play with some custom Production settings in a bit. For now, enjoy your progress. Believe it or not, you are now a published eLearning author. Congratulations!

5. Close the media player.

6. Review the Production Results.

   The **Production Results** dialog box contains some important information about your rendered project, including the location of the produced file and the size of the video.

```
Files created:
    ShareMe_MP4_Only.mp4

Content duration:  00:01:08 (hh:mm:ss)
Content size:      4.48 MB
Video Dimensions:  1280x720
Total Dimensions:  1280x720

Production Options:
Frame Rate:        30
Keyframe rate:     5
Pause at start:    Disabled
Bitrate Mode:      Quality Mode
H264 Profile:      Main
H264 Level:        Auto
Video Quality:     60 %
Audio Bitrate:     128 kbps
Audio Format:      AAC
Watermark:         Disabled
```

7. Click the **Open production folder** button.

Open production folder

   The **ShareMe_MP4_Only** folder opens. This folder contains the video you'll need to deliver to your learner.

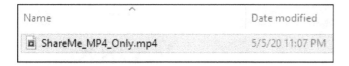

Name	Date modified
ShareMe_MP4_Only.mp4	5/5/20 11:07 PM

8. Close the **ShareMe_MP4_Only** window.

9. Click the **Finish** button on the Production Results dialog box. (Keep the project open for the next activity.)

NOTES

Guided Activity 37: Create a Web Video on the PC

1. Ensure that the **ShareMe** project is open.

2. Produce a video for the web that includes the Smart Player.

   ☐ choose **Share > Local File**

   The Production Wizard appears again.

   ☐ from the drop-down menu, **MP4 with Smart Player (up to 720p)**

   ☐ click the **Next** button

   ☐ name the Production file **ShareMe_SmartPlayer**

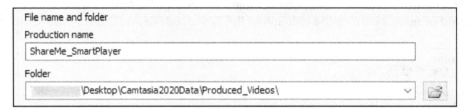

   ☐ click the **Finish** button

   Once rendered, the lesson does not open in the Media Player like last time. This time it opens in your default Web browser.

   ☐ click the **Play** button in the middle of the screen to play the lesson

   The Smart Player appears at the bottom of the window every time you move your mouse within the browser window. The player automatically disappears when you move your mouse away from the browser window.

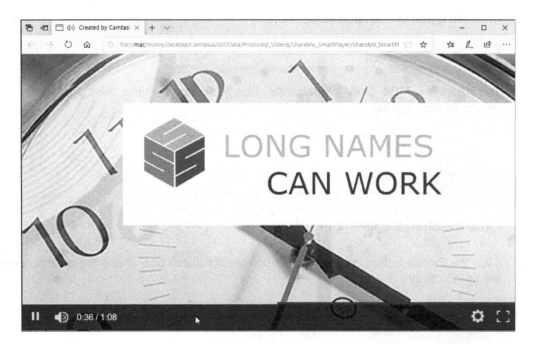

3. Close the browser window to close the lesson.

4. On the Production results screen, click the **Open production folder** button.

   When you published a standalone video, the production folder contained only one file (the MP4 video). Publishing content as web video results in several output files. Because this output is expected to work on desktop computers, laptops, and mobile devices, more files are needed to ensure the content loads correctly in the browser and can remain potentially interactive (interactivity includes such things as quizzes and hotspots, which you will learn about later). *All of the files in the output folder are required for the lesson to play/display correctly for your learner.*

Name	Date modified	Type	Size
scripts	5/5/20 11:18 PM	File folder	
skins	5/5/20 11:18 PM	File folder	
ShareMe_SmartPlayer.html	5/5/20 11:18 PM	HTML File	1 KB
ShareMe_SmartPlayer.mp4	5/5/20 11:18 PM	MP4 File	4,597 KB
ShareMe_SmartPlayer_config.xml	5/5/20 11:18 PM	XML File	3 KB
ShareMe_SmartPlayer_embed.css	5/5/20 11:18 PM	Cascading Style S...	1 KB
ShareMe_SmartPlayer_First_Frame.png	5/5/20 11:17 PM	PNG File	6 KB
ShareMe_SmartPlayer_player.html	5/5/20 11:18 PM	HTML File	7 KB
ShareMe_SmartPlayer_Thumbnails.png	5/5/20 11:17 PM	PNG File	0 KB

   In the image above, the *start page* is highlighted. The start page, which is an html file, was automatically created when you shared (rendered) the project. The start page is always given the name you used when you use the Share feature.

   Although all of the files in this folder are co-dependent and must be uploaded to the server, the start page is the page your learners need to start the video you rendered. If you are working with a webmaster or IT support, they need to understand the importance of keeping these files together *and* making the start page the target of any links to the course content within the folder you rendered.

5. Close the production window.

6. Back in Camtasia, click the **Finish** button to close the Production Results screen.

Guided Activity 38: Add a Watermark to PC Projects

1. Ensure that the **ShareMe** project is open.

2. Add a watermark.

   ☐ choose **Share > Local File**

   ☐ select **Custom production settings** from the drop-down menu

   ☐ click the **Next** button

   ☐ ensure that **MP4 - Smart Player (HTML5)** is selected

   ☐ click the **Next** button

   Among other things, this second screen allows you to disable the controller (the play bar) if you'd like. You'll leave the default settings.

   ☐ click the **Next** button again

3. Add a watermark.

   ☐ from the **Watermark** area, select **Include watermark**

   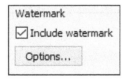

   ☐ click the **Options** button just below **Include watermark**

   The Watermark options appear along with a Watermark Preview window.

   ☐ click the **Browse** button at the right (the yellow folder)

   ☐ from the **Camtasia2020Data > Image_Files** folder, open **ForReviewOnly**

The image appears, by default, in the lower right of the Watermark Preview.

4. Change the position of the watermark.

    ❏ from the **Position** area, click the **top right** square (you may need to move the Watermark Preview window out of the way to see the Position area)

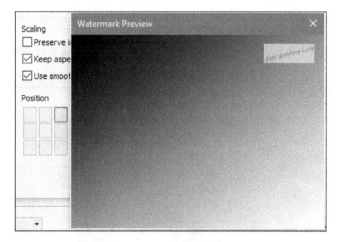

5. Remove the watermark's background color.

    ❏ from the **Effects** area, select **Use transparent color**

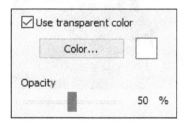

The background color behind the logo has been removed.

6. Change the Image scale.

    ❏ from the **Image scale** area, drag the slider until the scale changes to **30%**

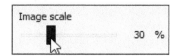

☐ click the **OK** button

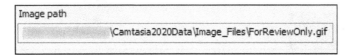

Image path

\Camtasia2020Data\Image_Files\ForReviewOnly.gif

☐ click the **Next** button to move to the final screen

7. Give the rendered video a new production name.

☐ change the **Production name** to **ShareMe_watermark**

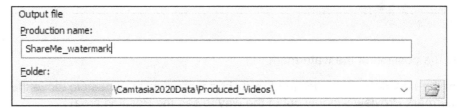

Output file

Production name:

ShareMe_watermark

Folder:

\Camtasia2020Data\Produced_Videos\

☐ click the **Finish** button

After rendering, the video (including the watermark), opens in your default web browser.

8. Close the browser.

9. Back in Camtasia, close the Production Results dialog box (click the **Finish** button).

10. Save your work.

Guided Activity 39: Share to YouTube

1. Ensure that the **ShareMe** project is open.

   Before you can share a video on YouTube, you will need a YouTube account. If you do not already have a YouTube or Gmail account, go to **www.youtube.com** or **gmail.com** now and set one up (it takes only a few moments and is free).

2. Share a video directly to YouTube.

   ☐ choose **Share > YouTube**

   You'll be prompted to Sign in to your YouTube account.

   ☐ click the **Sign In** button and then follow the onscreen prompts to access your YouTube account

3. Give the video a Title, Description, and Tags (keywords).

   ☐ in the **Title** field, type **Creating New Folders**

   ☐ in the **Description** field, type **This demonstration will teach you how to create a folder using Windows.**

   ☐ in the **Tags** field, type **training, windows, file management**

   The tags make it easier for YouTube users to search YouTube and find your video.

   ☐ leave the **Privacy** option set to **Public**

4. Share the video.

☐ click the **Finish** (PC) or **Share** (Mac) button

The video is rendered and automatically posted to your YouTube account.

5. Close the web browser and return to Camtasia.

Sharing Projects Confidence Check

If you work with a team of Camtasia developers, it's likely that you will be asked to share your project with team members so they can modify the project on their own. Sharing projects among developers is not the same as using the Share menu to render output for a learner as you've learned to do during this module.

To share a project with other Camtasia developers using different operating systems, follow these steps:

Windows to Mac: If you want to share a Windows-based project with someone who is using Camtasia 2020 for the Mac, choose **File > Export > Project for Windows**.

Mac to Windows: If you want to share a Mac-based project with someone who is using Camtasia 2020 for Windows, choose **File > Export > Project for Mac**.

Share Projects Mac to Mac: Sharing a project with other Mac developers is simple. When saving the project, ensure that you select **Create standalone project**. Send a team member the project file (the **cmproj** file), and you're set. The **cmproj** file is a self-contained collection of all project assets. If team members have the same or newer version of Camtasia as you, they'll be able to open and edit the project.

Share Projects PC to PC: PC projects are not self-contained projects like they are on the Mac. Assets added to the Media Bin are **linked** to their original location. When you import media into Camtasia from a local or network drive and then send just the Camtasia project file to someone outside your network, that person is prompted to locate the linked media as the project opens. If the missing media cannot be found, the project is essentially useless. Here are the steps necessary to share projects between PCs.

Note: The steps below are for PC users only. Mac users can save and close the project and then skip ahead to the next module which begins on page 115.

1. Choose **File > Export > Zipped Project**.

2. Browse to a save destination of your choice.

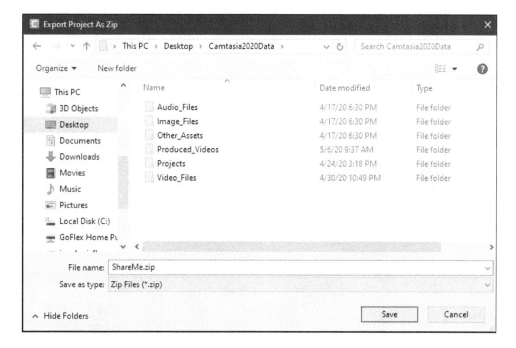

3. Click the **Save** button.

   The resulting zip file contains the Camtasia project and all of the project's assets. Assuming the recipient of the zip file has the same version of Camtasia as you, developers can extract the contents, open, edit, and share the project.

ShareMe.zip

2Step1.mp3 Type: MP3 File		Date modified: 6/20/18 8:07 AM Size: 0.97 MB → 0.97 MB
audio_file01.wav Type: WAV File		Date modified: 6/20/18 8:07 AM Size: 1.09 MB → 1.09 MB
audio_file02.wav Type: WAV File		Date modified: 6/20/18 8:07 AM Size: 1.48 MB → 1.48 MB
audio_file03.wav Type: WAV File		Date modified: 6/20/18 8:07 AM Size: 3.93 MB → 3.93 MB
audio_file04.wav Type: WAV File		Date modified: 6/20/18 8:07 AM Size: 3.13 MB → 3.13 MB
CreateNewFolderVideo.trec Type: TREC File		Date modified: 6/20/18 8:07 AM Size: 574 KB → 574 KB
logo.png Type: PNG File		Date modified: 6/20/18 8:07 AM Size: 15.5 KB → 15.5 KB
mainart.jpg Type: JPG File		Date modified: 6/20/18 8:07 AM Size: 324 KB → 324 KB
ShareMe.tscproj Type: TSCPROJ File		Date modified: 5/6/20 10:04 AM Size: 139 KB → 139 KB

---

4. Save the project.

iCONLOGiC
"Skills and Drills" Learning

Module 7: Extending, Zooming, and Hotspots

In This Module You Will Learn About:

And You Will Learn To:

Extending

If you record a software demonstration and then import audio into the project later, as you've done several times during the previous activities, synchronizing the video with the voiceover audio can be challenging. During the following activity, you'll learn how to freeze a video on a single frame, making synchronization easier.

Guided Activity 40: Extend a Video Frame

1. Open **ExtendZoomMe** from the Camtasia2020Data Projects folder.

2. On the Timeline, notice that **audio_file07** has been added to the Timeline at the **2:26;00 second mark**, above the **RestoreFolder** media.

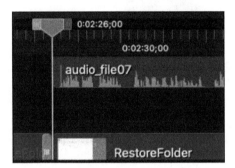

3. Beginning at **2:26;00** on the Timeline, Preview the video.

   In the video, the narrator is talking about the Recycle Bin and how its appearance has changed to indicate there's trash to be emptied. The video is just a bit ahead of the voiceover audio. Rather than re-record the video, you're going to freeze the video just long enough to synchronize the voiceover audio with the video.

4. Lock the **Voiceover** and **Background** tracks. (The video is in the Main track. As you learned on page 89, locking tracks prevents accidental changes to those tracks.)

5. Split a video into two segments.

   ❏ on the **Timeline**, zoom a bit closer to the **2:26;00** mark

   ❏ on the **Timeline**, drag the **Playhead** a bit right to **2:26;16**

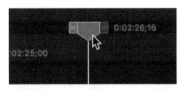

   This is the point in the video just before the cursor moves toward the Recycle Bin.

   ❏ on the **Timeline**, select the **RestoreFolder** media

   ❏ right-click the **Playhead** and choose **Split Selected**

   The video has been split into two segments.

6. Reposition a video segments.

☐ on the **Timeline**, position the **Playhead** at **2:29;05**

☐ drag the **larger** of the two video segments **right** until it snaps to the Playhead's position at **2:29;05**

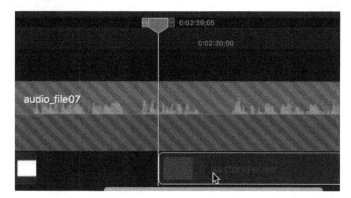

The gap between the two video segments, shown in the image above, is going to be filled by extending the last frame in the smaller segment. The process of extending a frame is a bit different between the Mac and PC versions of Camtasia. The steps for the Mac appear first, followed by the steps for the PC.

☐ Mac users, leave the **Playhead** positioned at **2:29;05**, select the first part of the split video (the smaller segment) and choose **Edit > Playhead > Extend Frame to Playhead**

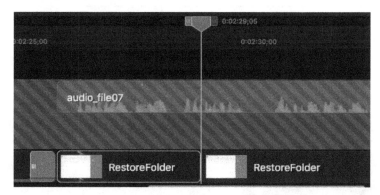

☐ PC users, double-click the **smaller video segment** to select it and move the Playhead in front of the segment

☐ right-click the segment and choose **Extend Frame**

☐ type **2.63** and click the **OK** button

7. All users, Preview the video from the beginning of the first RestoreFolder media segment.

Extending the frame has slowed down the video just enough so that the screen actions and voiceover audio are pretty well synchronized.

Zoom Animations

The Zoom-n-Pan feature is useful if the width and height of your project are large and you want to focus the learner's attention on a specific area of the screen. Zooming moves the learner closer to the screen; Panning automatically moves the screen for the learner. Adding Zooms and Pans is as simple as positioning the Playhead where you want to add the effect, accessing the Zoom-n-Pan panel (via Animations) and stretching and/or moving the Zoom-n-Pan window.

Guided Activity 41: Add a Zoom-n-Pan Animation on the PC

1. Ensure that the **ExtendZoomMe** project is open.

2. Add a Zoom-n-Pan mark.

   ☐ on the **Timeline**, position the Playhead at **0:47;27**

   On the Canvas, this is the moment in the video when the mouse pointer has arrived at the Home tab and is about to click.

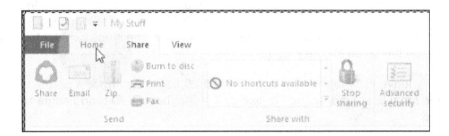

   ☐ from the list of tools at the left, click **Animations**

   There are two tabs: **Zoom-n-Pan** and **Animations**.

   ☐ select the **Zoom-n-Pan** tab

   ☐ on the **Zoom-n-Pan** panel, drag the lower right resizing handle **up** and to the **left** similar to the picture below

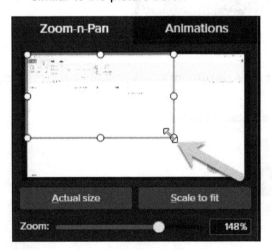

   When you drag the resizing handle on the Zoom-n-Pan panel, the Canvas displays how close you've actually gotten to the screen.

On the Timeline, notice that the Pan effect is represented by an arrow with two circles. You can change the zoom percentage by clicking the larger circle and changing the Scale on the Properties panel.

3. On the **Timeline**, position the **Playhead** a few seconds to the left of zoom effect you just added.

4. Preview the video.

   Thanks to the Zoom-n-Pan, you are automatically taken closer to the action in the video.

5. Save your work.

   The next activity is for Mac users only. PC users, skip ahead to the "Add a Timeline Marker" activity that begins on page 122.

Guided Activity 42: Add a Zoom Animation on the Mac

1. Ensure that the **ExtendZoomMe** project is open.

2. Add a Zoom-n-Pan mark.

   ☐ on the **Timeline**, unlock the locked tracks

   ☐ position the Playhead at **47;27**

   This is the area of the video where the mouse pointer has arrived at the Home tab and is about to click.

   ☐ from the list of tools at the left, click **Animations**

   ☐ from the list of Animations, drag the **Custom** animation to the **Timeline**

   ☐ position the animation on the **Creating Folders** group at **47;27**

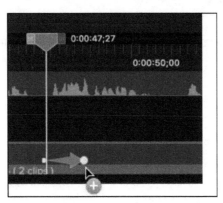

   On the Timeline, notice that the animation is represented by an arrow with two circles. The first (smaller) circle represents the beginning of the animation. The second circle represents the end of the animation. You can change the zoom percentage by clicking the larger circle and changing the Scale on the Properties panel.

   ☐ on the Timeline, select the animation icon's larger circle

☐ on the Properties panel, change the **Scale** to **200**

☐ on the **Canvas**, drag the video down and to the right so you can see the top left of the video

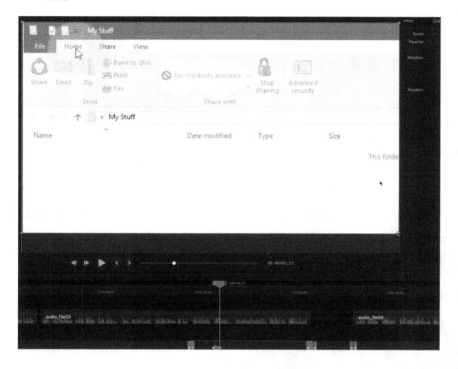

3. On the **Timeline**, position the **Playhead** a few seconds to the left of the zoom Animation you just added.

4. Preview the video.

   Thanks to the animation, you are automatically taken closer to the action in the video.

5. Save your work and close the project.

Markers

Markers are project-wide breadcrumbs that can be added to the Timeline or Timeline objects. Markers are the key to Camtasia's interactive features, such as a table of contents, closed captions, hotspot functionality, and quizzing.

Guided Activity 43: Add a Timeline Marker

1. Open **MarkMe** from the Camtasia2020Data Projects folder.

   On the Timeline, notice that there are some additional tracks: Nav1, Nav2, and Nav3. The tracks contain shapes at Timeline position 03;24.

2. Add and rename a Timeline Marker.

   ❏ on the **Timeline**, position the **Playhead** near the beginning of the video (at 00;23)

   ❏ choose **Modify > Markers > Add Timeline Marker**

   On the Timeline, a marker is added just below the Playhead. On the Properties panel, the new marker is named **Marker**.

   ❏ on the **Properties** panel, change the **Marker name** to **Home**

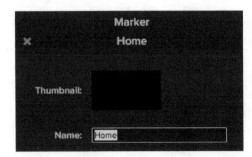

Markers and TOC Confidence Check

1. Still working in the **MarkMe** project, position the Playhead just after the transition for the **Lesson 1** group (05;15).

2. Add a new Timeline marker (**Modify > Markers > Add Timeline Marker**) named **Lesson 1: Creating New Folders**.

3. Position the Playhead at the **Lesson 2** group. (01:03;28)

4. Add a new Timeline marker named **Lesson 2: Renaming Folders**.

5. Position the Playhead at the **Lesson 3** group.

6. Add a new Timeline marker named **Lesson 3: Recycling and Restoring**. (01:45;23)

The Timeline should now have four markers.

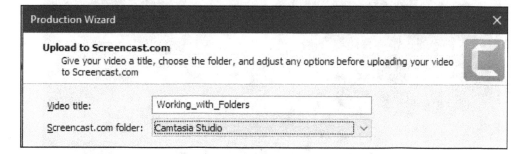

TechSmith provides a free service called Screencast where you can share your Camtasia output. Screencast is especially useful if you do not have a LMS or web server where you can host your shared output. You will need to create an account on Screencast.com prior to finishing this Confidence Check. If you do not have an account, go to **www.screencast.com** and set one up prior to moving to the next step.

7. Share a project to **Screencast.com** by choosing **Share > Screencast.com**.

8. Title the course **Working_with_Folders**.

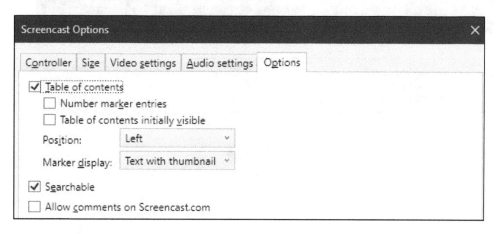

9. **PC users**, click the **Options** button and then select the **Options** tab. Ensure **Table of contents** is selected and click the **OK** button

Mac users, deselect **Include Quiz** and ensure **Create table of contents from markers** is selected.

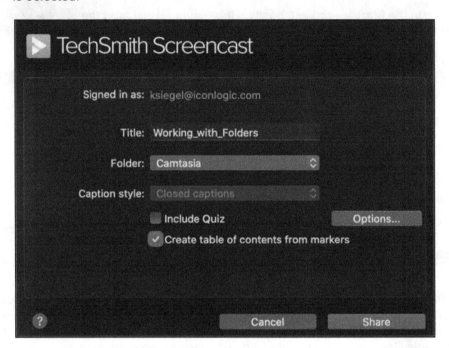

10. **Mac users,** click the **Share** button. Then click the **Visit** button to see the output on Screencast.com.

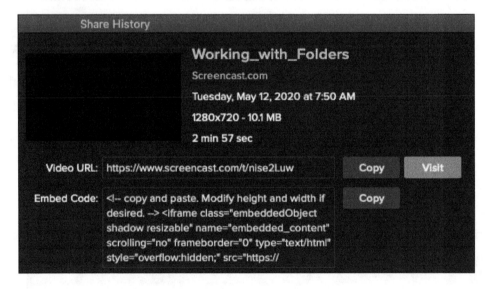

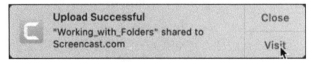

PC users, click the **Next** button and deselect Report quiz results through email (this option is not needed because there is not a quiz in the project) and click the **Finish** button

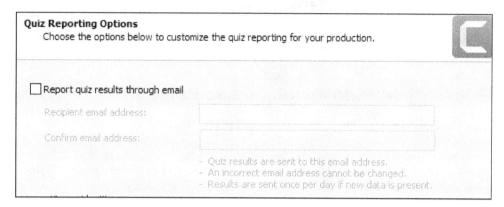

11. **PC users,** view the Shared project on Screencast.com.

    All users: On Screencast.com, the Table of Contents can be viewed by clicking the icon on the playbar at the bottom of the lesson. On the TOC, you can click any of the thumbnails to jump to the Timeline markers.

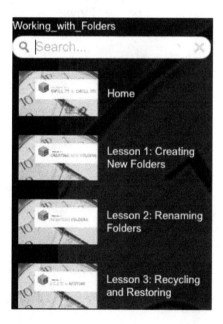

    Note: If the TOC does not work for you, try copying the web address in the browser's address bar and pasting it into the address bar within a different browser. On my Mac, Chrome works better than Safari.

12. Close the browser and return to Camtasia.

13. Close all open windows.

14. Save your work. (Mac users, you can save and close any open projects.)

NOTES

Hotspots

To maximize the effectiveness of your eLearning videos, you can use hotspots to add interactivity. The hotspots can pause the video and wait for a click from your learner. Once clicked, a hotspot can be set up to take the learner to a marker, a website, or a specific time on the Timeline.

Guided Activity 44: Add an Interactive Hotspot

1. Open **HotSpotMe** from the **Camtasia2020Data > Projects** folder.

   There are three shapes (shown in the image below) on the Canvas and at the beginning of the Timeline in the **Nav1**, **Nav2**, and **Nav3** tracks. You're going to use a hotspot to make each shape interactive.

2. Add an Interactive Hotspot to an object on the Canvas.

   ☐ zoom a bit closer to the **Timeline**

   ☐ on the **Timeline**, **Nav1** track, double-click the **green shape** at **03;28**

   The green annotation containing the number **1** is displayed on the Canvas and selected.

   ☐ from the tools at the left, click **Visual Effects**

   ☐ right-click **Interactive Hotspot** and choose **Add to Selected Media**

   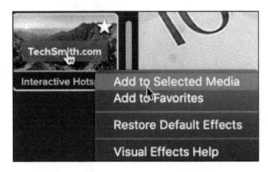

3. Add an Action to a Hotspot.

   ☐ on the **Properties** panel, **Interactive Hotspot** section, ensure **Pause at end** is selected

   This option ensures that the video doesn't move forward without giving the learner a chance to click the shape.

   ☐ on the **Properties** panel, **Interactive Hotspot** section, select **Marker**

☐ from the Marker drop-down menu, choose **Lesson 1: Creating New Folders** (you learned how to create this particular marker on page 122)

4. Save your work.

Interactive Hotspot Confidence Check

1. Add an Interactive Hotspot to the red annotation in the Nav2 track.

2. Make the target of the hotspot the **Lesson 2** marker.

3. Add an Interactive Hotspot to annotation in the Nav3 track.

4. Make the target of the hotspot the **Lesson 3** marker.

5. Share the project to **Screencast.com** with the Title **Working_with_Folders_Hotspots**.

6. Visit the lesson on Screencast.com and test the hotspots.

7. When finished, close the browser and then return to Camtasia.

8. Save your work. (Mac users, you can close the project.)

Notes

iCONLOGiC

"Skills and Drills" Learning

Module 8: Quizzes and Reporting Results

In This Module You Will Learn About:

- Quizzes, page 130
- Emailing Quiz Results, page 136
- Reporting Results, page 139

And You Will Learn To:

- Add a Quiz to a Project, page 130
- Add a Multiple Choice Question, page 132
- Add a Fill In the Blank Question, page 133
- Send Quiz Results via Email with Screencast.com, page 136
- Create a Content Package on the PC, page 139
- Create a Content Package on the Mac, page 142

Quizzes

Many people compare eLearning to live training. But it's not a fair comparison because eLearning lacks live, human interaction. In an instructor-led class, virtual or onsite, an experienced trainer can gauge the effectiveness of a lesson by asking the learner a question about something taught in the class. When a trainer asks questions, the learner has an opportunity to share what was learned and to prove demonstrate comprehension.

Although an eLearning lesson cannot provide live trainer-to-learner interaction, you can still engage the learner by adding a quiz to a Camtasia project. Each quiz can contain any or all of the following question types: Multiple choice, True/False, Fill in the blank, and Short answer.

Guided Activity 45: Add a Quiz to a Project

1. Open **QuizMe** from the Camtasia2020Data Projects folder.

2. Add a Quiz to the Timeline.

   ☐ on the **Timeline**, position the **Playhead** just after the last group (at **2:57;17**)

   ☐ from the list of tools at the left, click **Interactivity**

   ☐ on the **Interactivity** panel, click **Timeline**

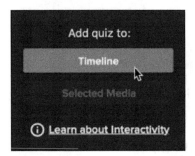

A Quiz marker is added to the Timeline and a Quiz Placeholder appears on the Canvas.

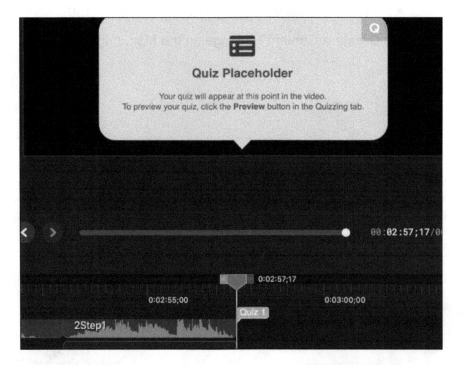

3. Rename the quiz.

   ☐ on the **Properties** panel, click **Quiz Options** (it's called **Quiz Option Properties** on the Mac, as shown in the second image below)

   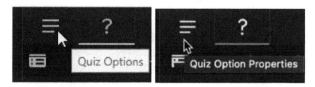

   ☐ change the Quiz Name to **Folders Quiz**

4. Ensure that the quiz will score the quiz questions.

   ☐ from just above the **Preview** button, ensure that **Viewers can see their results** is selected

   ☐ ensure that **Score Quiz** is selected

   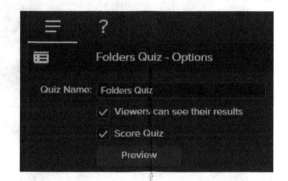

Guided Activity 46: Add a Multiple Choice Question

1. Ensure that the **QuizMe** project is open.

2. Add a Multiple Choice question to the quiz.

   ☐ on the **Properties** panel, click **Quiz Question Properties**

   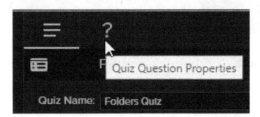

   ☐ from the **Type** drop-down menu, choose **Multiple Choice**

3. Type the question text.

   ☐ in the Question area, replace the placeholder text with **When giving a folder a name, how many characters can you use?**

4. Add four answers to the question.

   ☐ in the first Answer area, type **9**

   ☐ in the next Answer area, type **255**

   ☐ in the next Answer area, type **11**

   ☐ in the next Answer area, type **218**

   Note: There is an extra "Add answer..." placeholder as shown in the image at the right. Unless you type something into the placeholder, the answer will not appear in the quiz.

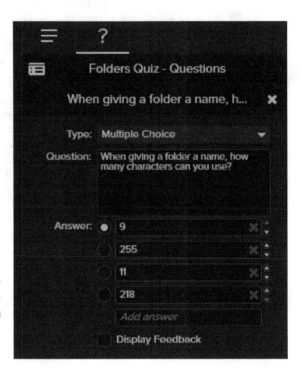

5. Specify a correct answer.

   ☐ click the circle next to the second answer, **255**

6. Save your work.

Guided Activity 47: Add a Fill In the Blank Question

1. Ensure that the **QuizMe** project is open.

2. Add a question.

   ☐ on the **Properties** panel, click **Add Question**

   The new question appears below the first.

3. Specify the question type.

   ☐ from the **Type** drop-down menu, choose **Fill in the Blank**

4. Edit the question.

   ☐ replace the Question Text placeholder text with **The New Folder icon is found on the ____ tab of the Ribbon.**

5. Edit the Answer.

   ☐ in the **Answer** area, replace the placeholder text with **Home**

   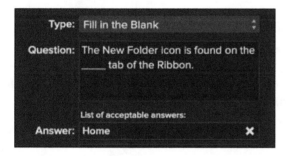

6. Save your work.

Quiz Confidence Check

1. Preview the quiz by clicking **See how Quiz looks in your viewer**. (On the Mac, the option is called **Preview quiz** as shown in the second image below.)

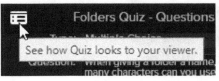  

A preview of the quiz appears on the Canvas.

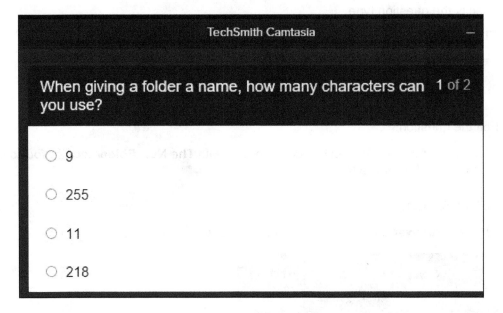

2. Select any of the answers in the first question and click the **Next** button (you'll likely need to scroll down to see the Next button).

3. Type anything you'd like into the text field within the **Fill in the Blank** question and then click the **Submit Answers** button.

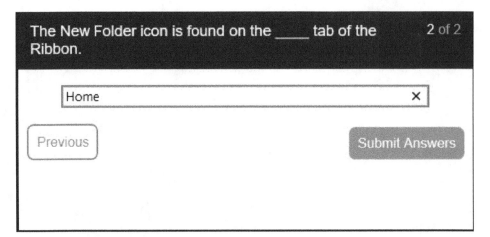

4. Click the **View Answers** button.

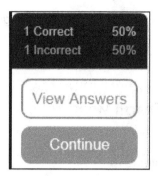

Correct answers are shown with a green check mark. Wrong answers are flagged with a red X.

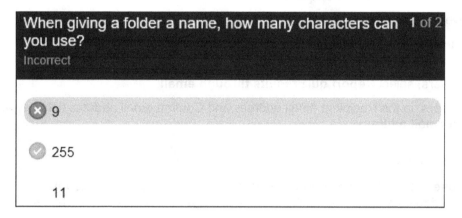

5. Close the Quiz preview.

6. Save the project. (Mac users, you can also close the project.)

Emailing Quiz Results

You learned how to Share a project to Screencast.com during a Confidence Check on page 123. Beyond allowing you to simply upload your published Camtasia videos and interactive courses, Screencast.com also tests the functionality of a quiz and gets quiz results from your learners via email.

Guided Activity 48: Send Quiz Results via Email with Screencast.com

1. Open **ReportMe** from the Camtasia2020Data Projects folder.

2. Set up the Quiz Reporting Options to send the quiz results to you via email.

   ☐ choose **Share > Screencast.com**

   ☐ leave the Title as is

   ☐ **PC users**, click the **Next** button
   Mac users, click the **Options** button

   ☐ **All users**, select **Report quiz results through email**

   ☐ **All users**, in the Recipient email address and Confirm email address fields, type **your email address**

3. Require Viewer identity.

   ☐ **All users**, from the **Viewer identity** area, select **Require viewers to input name and email address**

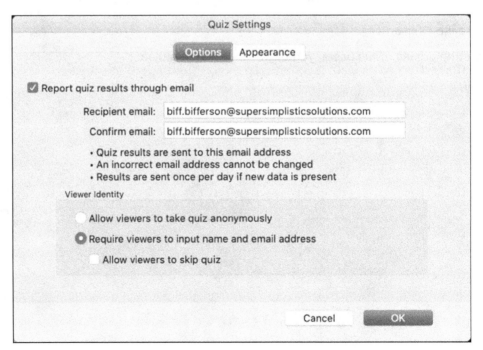

   ☐ **PC users**, click the **Finish** button
   Mac users, click **OK** button and then click the **Share** button

   The lesson is produced and then automatically uploaded into your Screencast account.

Screencast Confidence Check

1. **PC users:** Switch to your web browser. You should already be logged into Screencast.com. If so, move to the next step. If you are not logged into Screencast.com, use a web browser to access Screencast.com and login. Once logged in, your uploaded video automatically opens.

   Mac users: On the Share History window, click the Visit button.

2. Start the video, and you will be prompted to identify yourself (thanks to the **Viewer identity** option you selected a moment ago).

3. Fill in the fields with your first name, last name, and email address.

4. PC users, click the **Submit and Continue** button;
   Mac users, click the **Submit and View Quiz** button.

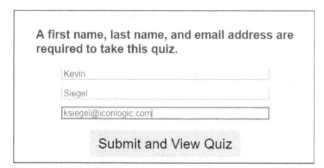

5. When the time comes to take the quiz, take it. You can answer the questions correctly or incorrectly.

6. After taking the quiz, continue through to the end of the video. When finished, close the browser.

7. If you have access to email, check your email. The quiz results should be sent to you from Camtasia Quiz Service. The email comes from services@techsmith.com. If you don't see the email, you might want to check your SPAM folder and/or add TechSmith to your server's White List. (Also, it was several hours before I received my first email from TechSmith.)

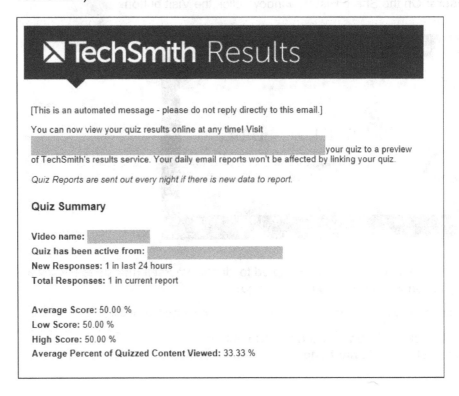

The Quiz results include a summary containing the number of responses, the average score, the low score, and the high score. Specific details about the quiz results are included as CSV files that can be opened with Microsoft Excel or other spreadsheet applications. The CSV files contain details about who took the quiz, the questions they got right and wrong, etc.

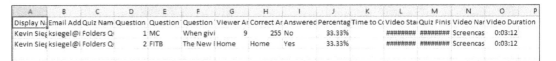

A	B	C	D	E	F	G	H	I	J	K	L	M	N	O	P
Display N	Email Add	Quiz Nam	Question	Question	Question	Viewer Ar	Correct Ar	Answerec	Percentag	Time to Co	Video Star	Quiz Finis	Video Nar	Video Duration	
Kevin Sieg	ksiegel@i	Folders Q	1	MC	When givi	9	255	No	33.33%	########	########	Screencas	0:03:12		
Kevin Sieg	ksiegel@i	Folders Q	2	FITB	The New I	Home	Home	Yes	33.33%	########	########	Screencas	0:03:12		

8. Close the e-mail (there is no need to save or send the e-mail).

9. Back in Camtasia, close any open dialog boxes and save your work.

Reporting Results

Earlier in this module you uploaded content to Screencast.com and had the quiz results emailed to you. As an alternative to tracking quiz results through email, most eLearning developers upload their training courses into a LMS. At a minimum, an LMS tracks learner access to the content, delivery of the content, and student performance tracking/reporting. Camtasia projects can be set up to report quiz scores to an LMS.

Prior to moving forward with setting up a project to the Shared output is appropriate for use within an LMS, I'd like to introduce you to two terms: SCORM and Manifests.

SCORM

SCORM is an acronym for Sharable Content Object Reference Model. Developed by public- and private-sector organizations, SCORM is a series of standards that specify ways to catalog, launch, and track course objects.

Courses and management systems that follow the SCORM specifications allow for sharing of courses among federal agencies, colleges, and universities. Although SCORM is not the only sharing standard, it is one of the most common. There are two primary versions of SCORM, both available in Camtasia: version 1.2, released in 1999, and version 2004.

Manifests

A Manifest allows your Shared output to be used and launched from a SCORM 1.2- or 2004-compliant LMS. When you Share a Camtasia project, you can have Camtasia create the Manifest file for you. The Manifest file that Camtasia creates contains XML tags that describe the organization and structure of the published project to the LMS.

During the activities that follow, you will create a content package, including a manifest file, suitable for upload into any SCORM-compliant LMS. The steps are different enough between the PC and Mac that I've split them up. PC users, you're up first below. Mac users, skip to page 142 for your steps to success.

Guided Activity 49: Create a Content Package on the PC

1. Ensure that the **ReportMe** project is still open.

2. Enable SCORM reporting.

   ☐ choose **Share > Local File**

   ☐ choose **Custom Production Settings** from the drop down menu

   ☐ click **Next** four times to advance to the **Quiz Reporting Options** screen

   ☐ deselect **Report quiz results through email**

   ☐ select **Report quiz results using SCORM**

☑ Report quiz results using SCORM
☐ Report quiz results through email

3. Set up the Manifest file.

   ☐ click the **SCORM Options** button

The Manifest Options dialog box opens.

☐ change the **Course Title** to **Computer Basics**

☐ add the following **Description** text: **This course will teach you everything you ever wanted to know about computers but were afraid to ask.**

☐ change the **SCORM version** to **1.2**

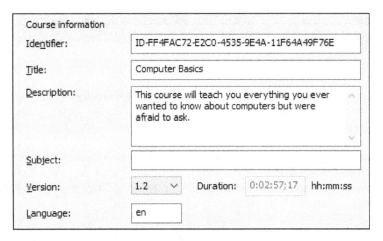

Some LMSs support SCORM version 1.2; some support only 2004, while others support both. Although it's typically a safe bet to go with SCORM 1.2, discuss the ideal version with your LMS vendor.

☐ change the **Lesson Title** to **Creating, Renaming, and Recycling Folders**

☐ from the **Quiz Success** area, set both values to **50%**

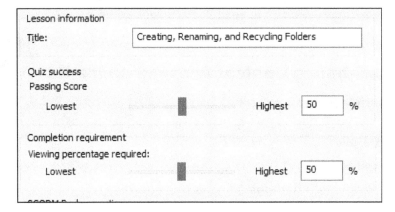

You have only two questions in your quiz, so a 50% pass setting seems about right.

☐ from the **SCORM Package options** area, select **Produce zip file**

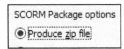

☐ click the **OK** button

You should be back on the Production Wizard.

☐ click the **Next** button

☐ change the Output file name to **ReportMeSCORM**

☐ ensure that the output folder is the **Camtasia2020Data > Produced_Videos**

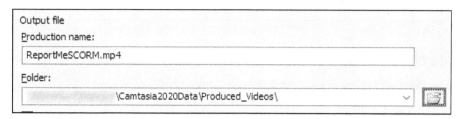

Output file

Production name:

ReportMeSCORM.mp4

Folder:

\Camtasia2020Data\Produced_Videos\

☐ click the **Finish** button

4. Once the rendering process is complete, click the **Open production folder** button.

    The zipped content package has been created, ready for you to upload into an LMS.

« Produced_Videos › ReportMeSCORM ›   ∨ ↻   Search Re... ⌕

Name	Type	Size
ReportMeSCORM.zip	WinZip File	11,090 KB

5. Close all windows.

6. Back in Camtasia, click the **Finish** button to close the Production results dialog box.

    The remaining steps in this module are for Mac users. You can move to the "PowerPoint, Captions, and Templates" module which begins on page 145.

NOTES

Guided Activity 50: Create a Content Package on the Mac

1. Ensure that the **ReportMe** project is still open.

2. Enable SCORM reporting.

   ☐ choose **Share > Local File**

   ☐ change the **Export As** file name to **ReportMeSCORM**

   ☐ ensure **Include Quiz** is selected

   ☐ select **Include SCORM**

3. Set up the Manifest file.

   ☐ to the right of **Include SCORM**, click the **Options** button

   The Manifest Options dialog box opens.

   ☐ change the **Course Title** to **Computer Basics**

   ☐ add the following **Description** text: **This course will teach you everything you ever wanted to know about computers but were afraid to ask.**

   ☐ change the **SCORM version** to **1.2**

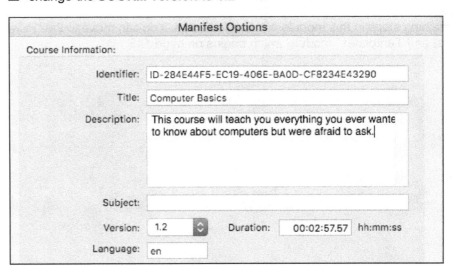

Some LMSs support SCORM version 1.2; some support only 2004, while others support both. Although it's typically a safe bet to go with SCORM 1.2, discuss the ideal version with your LMS vendor.

❏ change the **Lesson Title** to **Creating, Renaming, and Recycling Folders**

❏ from the **Quiz Success** area, set both values to **50%**

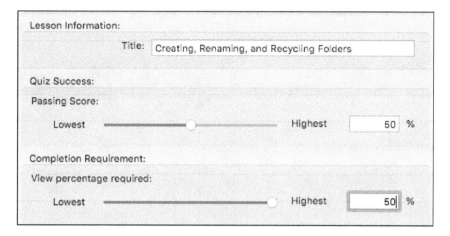

You have only two questions in your quiz, so a 50% pass setting seems about right.

❏ from the **SCORM Package options** area, select **Produce zip file**

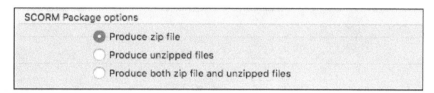

❏ click the **OK** button

❏ click the **Export** button

4. Once the Rendering process is complete, click the **Reveal in Finder** button.

The zipped content package has been created, ready for you to upload into an LMS.

5. Close all windows.

6. Back in Camtasia, save and close the project.

Notes

iCONLOGiC

"Skills and Drills" Learning

Module 9: PowerPoint, Captions, and Templates

In This Module You Will Learn About:

- PowerPoint to Camtasia, page 146
- Closed Captions, page 150
- Templates, page 166

And You Will Learn To:

- Record PowerPoint on the PC, page 146
- Import a PowerPoint Presentation, page 149
- Create PC Closed Captions, page 150
- Control PC Caption Timing, page 153
- Use Speech-to-Text to Create Captions, page 157
- Create Mac Closed Captions, page 159
- Control Mac Caption Timing, page 163
- Create and Use a Template, page 166

PowerPoint to Camtasia

I frequently meet eLearning developers who have created perfectly good Microsoft PowerPoint presentations, and they'd like to use those presentations as eLearning. Unfortunately, PowerPoint does not have the ability to add quizzes, create SCORM packages, or automatically upload content to YouTube or Screencast.com. Rather than try to recreate the PowerPoint presentation from scratch in Camtasia, you have two ways to re-purpose existing PowerPoint content in Camtasia. PC users can record a PowerPoint presentation from within PowerPoint using a Camtasia Add-in. The finished recording will end up in a Camtasia project as a video on the Timeline. From there, you can add all of the awesome Camtasia-specific features to the project that you've learned about in this book. Mac users cannot record a PowerPoint presentation from within PowerPoint because there isn't a Camtasia Recorder Add-in for the Mac version of PowerPoint. You can get around this limitation by recording your presentation using Camtasia's screen recorder (you learned how to use the Recorder on page 44).

Another option is to bring some or all the PowerPoint slides into Camtasia as images. Those images, which will be imported into the Media Bin, can then be added to the Camtasia Timeline.

You'll work with both options (recording using the PowerPoint recorder add-in) and importing PowerPoint as images) during the next few activities.

> **Note:** The next activity is for PC users only because the Camtasia add-in is not available on the Mac. **Mac users**, you can skip ahead to the activity on page 149.

Guided Activity 51: Record PowerPoint on the PC

1. If Camtasia is running, close the program.

2. Open a PowerPoint presentation with Microsoft PowerPoint.

   ☐ using Microsoft PowerPoint, open **S3_Policies** from the **Camtasia2020Data > Other_Assets** folder

   The Camtasia PowerPoint Add-in is automatically installed on your computer by the Camtasia application installer. Unless it has been disabled, you should be greeted with the dialog box below. (You can also confirm that the Camtasia Add-in has been installed by choosing **File > Options > Add-ins** from within PowerPoint.)

❑ click the **OK** button

❑ on the **Ribbon**, click the **Add-Ins** tab

Camtasia recording tools appear in the upper left of the PowerPoint window.

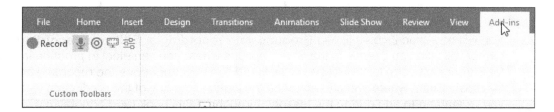

3. Record the PowerPoint presentation.

❑ from the **Custom Toolbars** area, click the **Record** tool

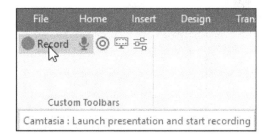

The PowerPoint slide show begins.

❑ in the lower right of the slide show, click the **Click to begin recording** button

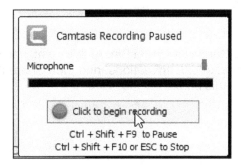

At this point, the presentation is being recorded, much like your screen was recorded when you learned to use Camtasia Recorder (on page 29).

❑ take your time and click in the middle of each slide to progress through the slide show

When you reach the end of the slide show, the alert dialog box shown below appears.

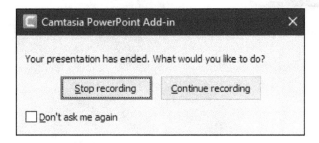

☐ click the **Stop Recording** button

You are prompted to save the recording.

☐ navigate to **Camtasia2020Data** folder

☐ open the **Video_Files** folder and then save the file

You will be asked if you'd like to **Produce your recording** or **Edit your recording**. The former will take you directly to the Share options where you can elect to produce the video for Screencast.com, for YouTube, or as HTML5. The latter opens the recording in the Camtasia Editor where you can enhance the video using any of the production techniques you've learned to add during the lessons throughout this book (add annotations, audio, quizzes, behaviors, images, videos, etc.).

☐ select **Edit your recording**

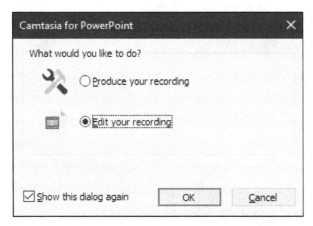

☐ click the **OK** button

The PowerPoint presentation is added to the Camtasia Media Bin. At this point, you could add the video to the Timeline, add annotations, audio, animations, and then Share the project as you have learned to do throughout this book.

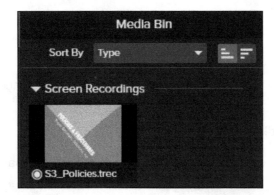

Guided Activity 52: Import a PowerPoint Presentation

1. **All users:** Create a new Camtasia project (there is no need to save previous projects).

2. Import PowerPoint slides into Camtasia as images.

   ☐ choose **File > Import > Media**

   ☐ from **Camtasia2020Data > Other_Assets**, open **S3_Policies**

   PC users, the PowerPoint slides are automatically added to the Media Bin as individual images. **Mac users,** you'll see a dialog box where you can elect to import all of the slides or select from a range of slides (you should import all of the slides).

   ☐ **Mac users:** click the **Import** button

Above, Mac users will see the option to import all of the PowerPoint slides or a range.

At the left, the imported PowerPoint slides appear on the Camtasia Media Bin.

Note: I sometimes receive "memory" error messages when attempting to import a PowerPoint presentation, even though my computer has plenty of memory. If the PowerPoint import process did not work or you received an error message, start PowerPoint prior to attempting to import the slides into Camtasia. Leave PowerPoint running until the import process is finished.

3. Add multiple images to the Timeline at one time.

   ☐ on the **Media Bin**, select any one of the images

   ☐ PC users, press [**ctrl**] [**a**] to select all of the images
   Mac users, press [**command**] [**a**] to select all of the images

   ☐ right-click any of one of the imported images and choose
   Add to Timeline at Playhead

Closed Captions

Closed captioning allows you to provide descriptive information in your published eLearning project that typically matches the voiceover audio in your Camtasia project.

There are a couple of ways you can add closed captions to a Camtasia project. The following activities show you how to add the captions manually (by transcribing) and how to create the Captions automatically via Speech-to-Text.

The process of creating closed captions is a bit different between the PC and Mac, so I've split them up. PC users, your activity appears below. Mac users, you can skip ahead to the "Create Mac Closed Captions" module which begins on page 159.

Guided Activity 53: Create PC Closed Captions

1. Open **CaptionMe** from the **Camtasia2020Data > Projects** folder. (When prompted to save the project from the last activity, there is no need to do so.)

   There are seven audio files in the **Voiceover** track. You'll need to listen to and then type the audio you hear as closed captions.

2. Open the Captions tool.

   ☐ choose **View > Tools > Captions**

3. Add captions manually.

   ☐ on the **Timeline**, position the **Playhead** at **5;00** (this is where the first voiceover audio clip is positioned)

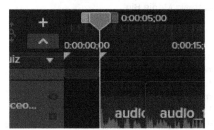

   ☐ on the **Canvas**, click the **Play** button and listen to the audio

   In this first audio segment, the narrator says: "Welcome to Super Simplistic Solutions learning series. This is lesson one: Creating New Folders."

   ☐ on the **Timeline**, re-position the **Playhead** at exactly **5;00**

   ☐ on the **Captions** panel, click **Add Caption**

   A callout is added to both Track 4 and the Canvas.

❑ on the **Canvas**, type the following into the Caption area:
Welcome to Super Simplistic Solutions learning series.

4. Format the Caption text.

❑ click the **Font Properties** drop-down menu 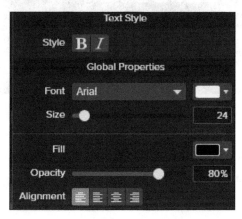 and change the **Size** to **24**

The Americans with Disabilities Act (ADA), a 1990 US civil rights law, prohibits discrimination against individuals with disabilities. Generally speaking, the ADA exists to ensure that people with disabilities have the same rights and opportunities as everyone else. The law guarantees equal opportunity for individuals with disabilities in public accommodations, employment, transportation, state and local government services, website experiences, and even eLearning.

When creating eLearning content, you should avoid doing anything in your project that does not conform to ADA standards. In the image below, the new Caption's font size is not ADA-compliant as indicated by the X to the right of the Font Properties drop-down menu.

5. Make Caption font formatting ADA-compliant.

☐ click the **ADA Compliance** drop-down menu

☐ click the **Make Compliant** button

The Caption's formatting conforms to ADA standards as indicated by the check mark.

6. Add another Caption.

☐ on the **Timeline**, position the Playhead to the right of the first Caption

☐ from the **Captions** panel, click the **Add Caption** button

☐ in the Caption area on the Canvas, type **This is lesson one: Creating New Folders.**

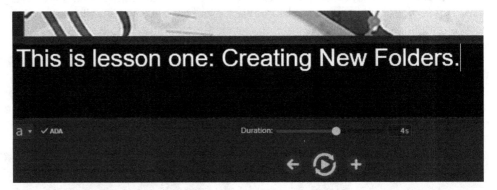

Guided Activity 54: Control PC Caption Timing

1. Ensure that the **CaptionMe** project is open.

2. Zoom closer to the Timeline.

3. On the **Timeline**, notice that the first Callout is onscreen about a second and a half too long. The vertical line in the image below indicates when the narrator has finished saying the word "series."

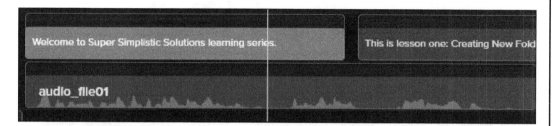

It's a best practice to synchronize the audio and the timing of the Captions. In this instance, you need to shorten the Caption's playtime.

4. Adjust Caption Timing

☐ on the **Timeline**, drag the **right** edge of the **first** Caption to the **left** a bit to shorten its play time

PC Captions Confidence Check

1. Move the second Caption left so it lines up with the audio as shown below.

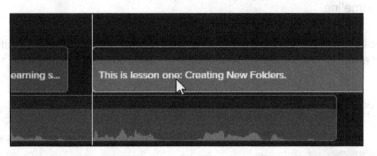

2. Shorten the playtime of the second Caption so it matches the audio.

3. Add a third caption just to the right of the first two containing this text: **This lesson is going to teach you how to create a new folder on your computer.**

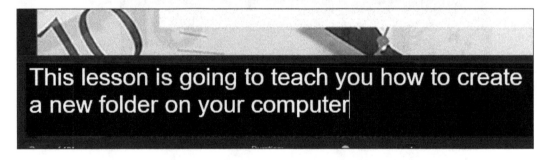

4. If necessary, make adjustments to the Caption's timing so it matches the audio as closely as possible.

5. Share the project as a Local File. (Select Custom Production Settings.)

6. Click the **Next** button until you get to the **Smart Player** Options.

---

7. Select the **Options** tab.

From this screen, you can enable or disable Captions and make their default state "visible" or "on by default." The standard is to make Captions not visible by default, so leaving **Captions initially visible** deselected is fine as is.

8. Click the remaining **Next** buttons and the **Finish** button to finish the rendering process.

9. View the video in your web browser.

10. Click the **CC** button to view the Captions.

11. Close the browser window.

12. Back in Camtasia, close the Production Results window.

As you've now learned, you can manually create Captions by typing them manually. Next you'll get a chance use text within a voiceover script as Caption content.

NOTES

13. Minimize Camtasia and, from the Camtasia2020Data, **Other_Assets** folder, open **CreatingFoldersVoiceoverScript** using Microsoft Word.

> ### Audio File 1:
> Welcome to Super Simplistic Solutions learning series.
> This is lesson one: Creating New Folders.
>
> ### Audio File 2:
> This lesson is going to teach you how to create a new folder on your computer, how to rename it, and how to both delete and restore recycled items.
>
> ### Audio File 3:
> When creating folders keep in mind that you can create as many folders as you need.

14. In the **Audio File 2** text section, select **"how to rename it, and how to both delete and restore recycled items"** and copy the text to the Clipboard.

15. Return to Camtasia and the **CaptionMe** project.

16. Position the Playhead just to the right of your existing Captions.

17. Create a new Caption and paste the text you copied into the space beneath the Canvas.

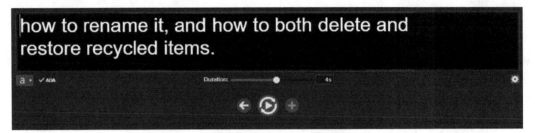

18. Save your work.

Guided Activity 55: Use Speech-to-Text to Create Captions

1. Ensure that the **CaptionMe** project is open.

2. On the **Timeline**, select and delete all of the Captions on **Track 4.**

3. Create Captions using Speech-to-Text.

   ☐ from the upper left of the **Captions** panel, click **Script Options** (the **gear** icon)

   ☐ choose **Speech-to-Text**

You'll receive some tips for improving the Speech-to-Text feature. Later, after you've had a chance to work with Camtasia, you should try some of these tips and see how they improve the Speech-to-Text results. For this activity, you're going to use the default settings and see where they take you.

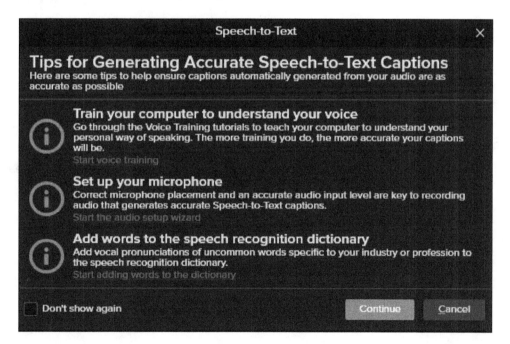

   ☐ click the **Continue** button

NOTES

Camtasia listens to the voiceover audio in the background and, like magic, creates Captions on Track 4.

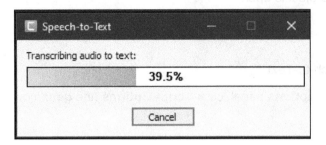

Look through the Timeline and notice in the image below that although much of the audio was transcribed nicely, many of the Captions need editing.

> this lesson is going to teach you how to create a new folder a new computer Halloween name it and how both the leap and restore recycled

You've now learned three ways to create Captions: transcribing, copy/paste from a script, and Speech-to-Text. The copy/paste technique is the most efficient way to create Captions, assuming there's a voiceover script. If there's no voiceover script, and you cannot afford to have the audio transcribed for you, the Speech-to-Text feature, given enough customization and tweaking, yields higher than average returns. Both techniques are faster than manually transcribing the audio tracks.

4. Save your work.

The next few activities on Captions are for Mac users. PC users, you can skip ahead to page 166 and learn about Templates.

Guided Activity 56: Create Mac Closed Captions

1. Save and close any open projects.

2. Open **CaptionMe** from the Camtasia2020Data Projects folder.

   There are several audio clips in the Voiceover track. You're going to listen to some of the clips and manually create a few Captions.

3. Add captions manually.

   ☐ from the tools at the left, click **Audio Effects**

   ☐ from the list of Audio Effects, drag **Captions** on top of the first audio clip in the Voiceover Track (on the Timeline)

   The Caption Track opens just above the Timeline.

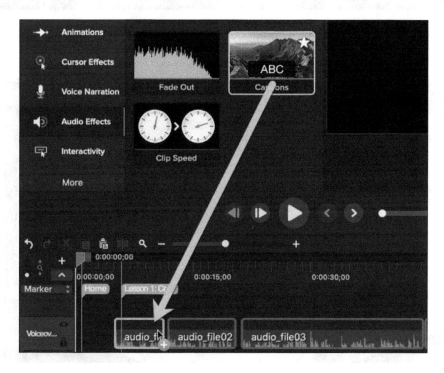

The Caption track opens just above the Timeline.

   ☐ on the **Caption track**, click the **left side** of the audio waveform

NOTES

The first part of the audio plays and a typing area opens. In this first audio segment, the narrator says: **Welcome to Super Simplistic Solutions learning series. This is lesson one: Creating New Folders.**

☐ type the following into the space beneath the background image: **Welcome to Super Simplistic Solutions learning series.**

The Caption you typed automatically appears on the Canvas. This is what learners will see if they view the lesson's closed captions.

4. Format the Caption text.

☐ on the **Caption track**, double-click the left side of the audio file

☐ on the Caption, click the **Change font properties for captions** tool

The Font options open.

❏ change the font size to **18**

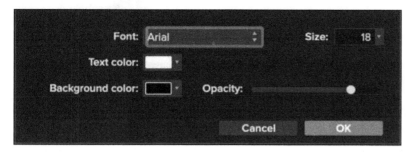

❏ click the **OK** button

On the Canvas, the change to the font size is immediate. Although the smaller font size might look better than the larger font, keep in mind that the Captions aren't necessarily for you—they're for learners who cannot hear the audio. When creating eLearning content, you'll need to be on the alert to anything you might do in your project that does not conform to the Americans with Disabilities Act (ADA).

In case you're not familiar with the ADA, it's a 1990 US civil rights law that prohibits discrimination against individuals with disabilities in all areas of public life, including jobs, schools, transportation, and all public and private places that are open to the general public. Generally speaking, the law exists to ensure that people with disabilities have the same rights and opportunities as everyone else and guarantees equal opportunity for individuals with disabilities in public accommodations, employment, transportation, state and local government services, and even eLearning.

In the case of font sizes used in Captions, a larger font is preferred because it is easier to see.

5. Restore the Caption's font size to its larger size.

   ❏ on the **Caption track**, click the left side of the audio file again

   ❏ click the **Change font properties for captions** tool

   ❏ change the font size back to **32**

   ❏ click the **OK** button

6. Add another Caption.

   ❏ on the **Caption track**, click the **right** side of the audio waveform

   ❏ type **This is lesson one: Creating New Folders.**

7. Preview the video from the beginning of the Timeline.

The captions appear, but they do not exactly match the voiceover audio. For instance, the first Caption is onscreen a bit too long. You'll fix that next.

Guided Activity 57: Control Mac Caption Timing

1. Ensure that the **CaptionMe.cmproj** project is open.

2. Adjust Caption Timing.

   ☐ on the **Caption track**, click the **left side** of the audio file

   ☐ on the Caption panel, change the **Duration** to **3** seconds

3. Preview the video from the beginning of the Timeline.

   The Caption timing is more in sync with the voiceover audio.

Mac Captions Confidence Check

1. Add a caption to the second audio file on the Timeline with the following text: **This lesson is going to teach you how to create a new folder on your computer.**

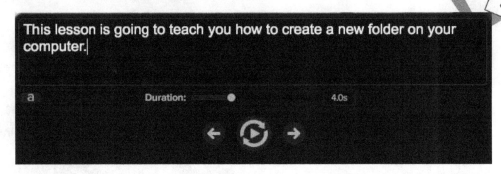

2. Share the project to Screencast.com. (Prior to clicking the Share button, choose **Closed captions** from the **Caption style** drop-down menu.)

3. After the Export process is complete, Visit the page on Screencast.com.

4. After starting the lesson, click the **CC** button on the playbar to view the Captions you added.

5. Close the browser window.

   Now you'll get a chance to copy and paste text from an existing voiceover script.

6. Hide Camtasia (to get it out of your way for a moment) and, from the Camtasia2020Data > **Other_Assets** folder, open **CreatingFoldersVoiceoverScript** with Microsoft Word.

> ### Audio File 1:
> Welcome to Super Simplistic Solutions learning series.
> This is lesson one: Creating New Folders.
>
> ### Audio File 2:
> This lesson is going to teach you how to create a new folder on your computer, how to rename it, and how to both delete and restore recycled items.
>
> ### Audio File 3:
> When creating folders keep in mind that you can create as many folders as you need.

7. In the **Audio File 2** text, select **"how to rename it, and how to both delete and restore recycled items"** and copy the text to the Clipboard.

8. Return to Camtasia and the CaptionMe project.

9. Still working in the section caption, click the right side of the waveform and paste the text you copied into the caption text area.

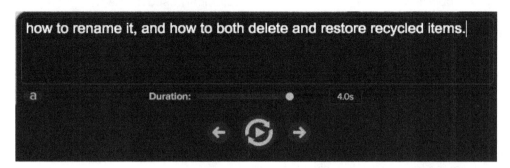

how to rename it, and how to both delete and restore recycled items.|

a   Duration: ●   4.0s

10. Save your work.

11. Close the project.

NOTES

Templates

Every time you create a new Camtasia project you're literally starting with a blank canvas. As you've learned during this book, it's easy to fill the Canvas with Library elements, images, annotations, videos, media, and add transitions to media. However, if there are assets and affects that you frequently use in your projects, it's not necessary to start from scratch every time. Instead, you should create a template that contains commonly used elements. When you create a Camtasia project that uses the template, all of the template's Timeline elements, behaviors, etc., will be retained, saving you all kinds of time as opposed to starting from scratch.

Guided Activity 58: Create and Use a Template

1. Create a new project.

2. Add a Library asset to the Timeline.

   ❏ from the tools at the left, click **Library**

   ❏ open the **Intros** folder

   ❏ right-click **Minimal Elegance Title 1** and choose **Add to Timeline at Playhead**

3. Add a placeholder.

   ❏ position the Playhead approximately **5 seconds to the right** of the Intro that you just added

   ❏ choose **Edit > Add Placeholder**

A Placeholder is an object that can be replaced with any piece of media from the Media Bin, Library, or Annotations. In this instance, the intent is for anyone using your template to replace the Placeholder with a screen recording. You'll add instructions next so that anyone using the Template knows what to do with the Placeholder.

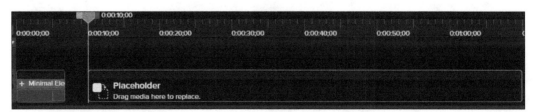

4. Edit Placeholder Properties.

☐ with the Placeholder selected, click in the **Title** area of the Placeholder Properties

☐ type **Screen Recording**

☐ click in the **Notes** field and type **Replace this Placeholder with a screen recording by dragging a video from the Media Bin here.**

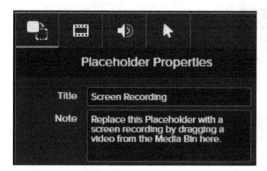

Notice that there's a gap between the two Timeline objects, indicated by the box in the image below.

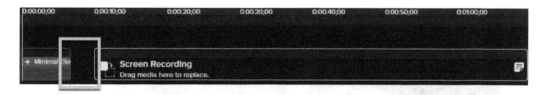

While you could easily drag the Placeholder left and remove the gap, there's a cool Camtasia feature called Magnetic Tracks that not only removes the gap but also ensures that there will not be any gaps in any projects that use your template (in this particular track).

5. Enable Magnetic Tracks.

☐ at the left of **Track 1** on the Timeline, click **Enable magnetic track**

The gap between the Timeline objects is removed.

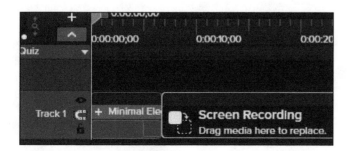

6. Save a project as a template.

    ☐ choose **File > Save project as template**

    The New Template dialog box opens.

    ☐ name the New Template **Recording Template**

    ☐ click the **OK** button

    PC users, You'll be alerted about how to use the template to create a new project. You can acknowledge the alert dialog box by clicking the **OK** button.

    Mac users, close the Untitled project without saving.

7. Create a project based on the new template.

☐ choose **File > New Project from Template**

The Template Manager opens.

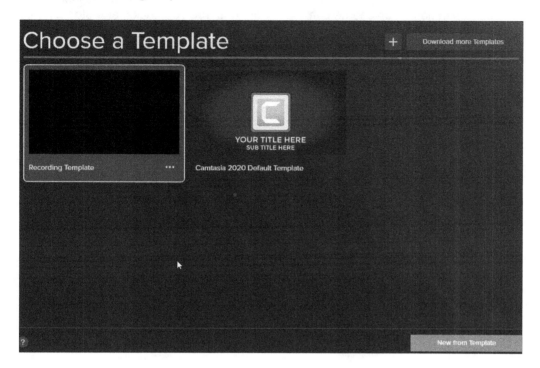

☐ select the **Recording Template** you just created

☐ click the **New from Template** button

PC users, you'll be prompted to save the project you used to build the Template. You can click the **No** button.

A new project is created that has all of the elements from your template. At this point you could replace the placeholder text and object with content of your own, just as you have learned to do during lessons throughout this book.

In the image below, I dragged a video from my Media Bin to the Placeholder. The video's playtime was far shorter than the placeholder. There are two options: **Ripple Replace** and **Replace with Clip Speed**. I selected Ripple Replace, which removed the excess playtime from the Placeholder.

8. Exit Camtasia. (There is no need to save any open files if prompted.)

And that's a wrap! I'd like to congratulate you on completing this book and wish you much success using TechSmith Camtasia to develop eLearning videos. I'm hoping you are now comfortable creating projects and project templates, recording software demonstrations, and adding assets such as videos, annotations, images, behaviors, audio, quizzes, and

captions. You should also feel comfortable in your ability to Share your content locally, on YouTube, and on Screencast.com.

If you need help using Camtasia, the first place to look for help is online via the TechSmith Camtasia website (http://techsmith.com) and TechSmith blog (blogs.techsmith.com). TechSmith has an awesome community offering free tips, tricks, and step-by-step videos covering all things Camtasia.

You can also email me at **ksiegel@iconlogic.com** if you need a nudge in the right direction, live, virtual Camtasia mentoring, or online or onsite training.

Index

NOTES

NOTES

Notes